What Oth
Greg Andersen and *Small Business Sales, Without The Fear*

"In *Small Business Sales, Without the Fear*, Greg Andersen removes the fear from sales. This is the perfect book for the small business owner who is trying to wear too many hats and isn't always able to get to the most important one—sales. Whether you decide to do sales yourself or you hire someone to help you, you'll find the answers you need in these pages to streamline your business and get the kinds of customers you crave."

— Tyler Tichelaar, PhD and award-winning author of *Narrow Lives* and *When Teddy Came to Town*

"Whether you're an accomplished salesperson or just trying to get your sole proprietorship afloat, in *Small Business Sales, Without The Fear*, you'll learn how to separate your fears and frustrations from what needs to be done to accomplish successful relationships with your customers. Practical, precise, and powerful advice fills every chapter, and once you read about and begin implementing the strategies in this book, you'll feel like it was always your destiny to succeed at small business sales!"

— Patrick Snow, Publishing Coach and International Best-Selling Author of *Creating Your Own Destiny* and *Boy Entrepreneur*

"Greg, I'm so glad to see that you have finally put your many years of experience in sales into a format that can now be shared with the world. This book is for sure a tool many of us entrepreneurs needed to attract, sell, and retain customers and clients."

— Seconde Nimenya, Author of *A Hand to Hold* and the International Award-Winning Memoir *Evolving Through Adversity*.

"So many people are afraid of sales, but the truth is that selling is easy when you approach it with the right attitude and a few fool-proof strategies to help solve your customers' problems rather than just sell to them. In *Small Business Sales, Without The Fear*, Greg Andersen teaches you how to do just that. Before you know it, you'll be stepping into your role as salesperson as if the sales shoes were made just for you."

— Nicole Gabriel, Author of *Finding Your Inner Truth* and *Stepping Into Your Becoming*

"Greg helped me to identify and fine-tune several different pros-pecting techniques that yielded good results. I was able to meet with 33 percent of the people I cold called! Greg's enthusiasm and knowledge of sales supported me in overcoming numerous chal-lenges. I would highly recommend Greg's book, *Small Business Sales, Without The Fear* if your goal is to maximize sales!"

— Robert Landis, Owner Capitol Media

SMALL BUSINESS
SALES
WITHOUT THE FEAR

NAVIGATING SALES & SELLING SOLUTIONS
FOR SMALL BUSINESS OWNERS

GREG ANDERSEN

AVIVA
PUBLISHING
New York

Small Business Sales, Without The Fear: The Small Business Owner's Guide to Creating Sales on Purpose

Address all inquiries to:
Greg W. Andersen
greg@smallbusinesssaleswtf.com
www.smallbusinesssaleswtf.com

Published by:
Aviva Publishing
Lake Placid, NY, USA
(515) 523-1320
www.AvivaPubs.com

ISBN: 978-1-63618-000-7
Library of Congress Control Number: 2020915311

Cover Design: Nicole Gabriel
Layout & Design: Nicole Gabriel
Editor: Janna Hiiva/Tyler Tichelaar

Every attempt has been made to source all quotes properly.
Printed in the United States of America
First Edition
1 2 3 4 5 6 7 8 9 10

For additional copies, bulk copies, or custom publishing opportunities, visit www.smallbusinesswtf.com.

For speaking engagements or to arrange a seminar, visit www.smallbusinesswtf.com.

ACKNOWLEDGMENTS

Throughout my life and my twenty-eight-year career, I have learned many things. But of all those things, one lesson is always at the top: We never do anything completely alone. No matter who we are, where we are, where we are going, or how we get there, we never, and I mean never, get there by ourselves.

Countless stories exist of "self-made" people and "lone-wolf" entrepreneurs, but if you look closely, eventually, you will always see that the people and circumstances in their lives made everything they accomplished possible. No one is a subject matter expert in all things. No one is born with the ability to create without some support from the good people around them. So I would like to take a moment to say thank you to a few people who have helped me realize my many dreams.

Dad and Mom (Better known as Gary and Mike Andersen): You inspired me from the very beginning to be who I want to be, create what I want to create, and try new things to expand my horizon. I'm not sure I ever heard the word "can't" from either of you, unless you were explaining to me "If you think you can, you can. If you think you can't, you can't. If you give up before you start, it is almost a cinch you won't." I have never really been bored because, as my father says, "Boredom is a state of mind…." I have never stopped dreaming because my mom never stopped enjoying my ideas, no matter how crazy they were/are.

Carrie, Cameron, and Kees: Living with an "idea guy" is never easy. My wife Carrie, my son Cameron, and my daughter Kees have been very patient with me over the years and that patience is how I was not only able to complete this book but achieve many things in my life. At the end of the day, you have to know when you come home at night that you are loved and supported. I have always felt both loved and supported even with some of my hair-brained ideas.

Bruce and Bob: Just out of college, I took my first sales position with Bruce Walker and Bob Valentine, the owners of Valco Graphics. Right out of college we don't usually get to pick the people we work with. Heck, I just wanted a job. But if you are fortunate enough to start off your career with people like Bruce and Bob, you have won the lottery. As mentors, leaders, salespeople, fathers, and friends, they had all the tools. I have patterned my career off of what Bruce and Bob taught me, and those lessons have probably had the most influence on my success.

Kurt Dammeier: My second job out of college was for a printing company called Print Northwest. The Dammeier family owned the business, but Kurt, the president, hired me and introduced me to a different side of both printing and sales. Kurt is one of the most talented salespeople I have ever met. His ability and enthusiasm are attributes I have tried to emulate.

Steve Brown: My third job out of college was with CDS in Medford, Oregon. The president, Steve Brown, provided me with an interesting spin on my career. Steve and I had not met until about eleven years into my career, but his influence was larger than he knows, and larger than I would like to admit. I have to preface what I am about to say by stating that I am giving Steve a compliment, even if it may not sound like it. Steve was my most challenging boss to date. He was my sales manager, my president, and often, my tormentor. While Steve possessed a tremendous intellect and an acute sense of how to win, our styles never really meshed. But one thing I learned early on was that you can learn from anyone. Steve taught me the art of thinking big, playing to win, and taking risks when necessary. As with so many things, I did not really appreciate Steve until years after I stopped working for him. He taught me that leading is not a popularity contest, to never give up, to improve all the time, and most importantly, to be prepared because life is a pop quiz.

Catherine McGavin: Catherine and I worked together at CDS for many years. Next to my father, who was a teacher for his entire career,

Catherine is probably the best teacher I know. We partnered on many accounts, and to this day, I look back fondly on our adventures, like the limousine ride in Tampa or playing possum in Las Vegas. While Steve Brown told me to be a consultative salesperson, Catherine demonstrated how to be a consultative sales professional. It was painful, it was hard, and she always supported my efforts, even when positive results did not materialize. She is a true friend and an excellent teacher.

Patrick Snow: I worked with Patrick as a speaker for his Best Selling Publishing Institute seminars. While I was simply helping teach his clients about how to deal with book printers, I absorbed knowledge and excitement about writing a book by simply being around Patrick. His ability to lead, motivate, and show that anything is possible if you simply believe is a big part of how I came to write this book. As a leader, he does not just teach; he is also a best-selling author, as you would expect. If you are interested in writing your own book, I highly recommend contacting Patrick at www.CreateYourOwnDestiny.com. Talking with and getting to know Patrick will change your life forever, even if you end up never writing a book!

As you can see, I am who I am based on hard work and the support, guidance, and patience of those I have been fortunate enough to have in my life. No one does anything alone.

To everyone I mentioned and to a whole lot of other customers and coworkers I have not mentioned, thank you. I dedicate this book to you.

Where do dreams come from? Where does courage come from? The courage and determination to chart your own path is often the reason many business owners decide to open, run, and grow their own businesses. If it were easy, low-risk, or problem free, everyone would do it.

If you are going to spend your life building your dream, you might as well spend a little time protecting your dream.

— Gregory W. Andersen

CONTENTS

PREFACE

I was a very shy child.

That I majored in speech communications and have spent the last twenty-eight years as an outside sales professional is, to this day, as baffling to me as it is to my parents. The only way I can explain it is that some people find their voice early in life, some find it later in life, and some never find it at all.

What most people do not really understand is that, even today, I consider myself somewhat shy. Those who know me will understand this. During the work week, I am on stage and do what I do. But, come the weekend, I am off stage and do not seek the attention or stimulus the outside sales jungle requires and provides.

Because I have spent my entire career in the printing industry, my stories, ideas, and perspectives in this book will all share this common thread. I decided to write this book because I've concluded that nearly everything I've learned over the last twenty-eight years is relevant from a sales point of view to almost every business and industry. I realized I was less in the printing industry and more in the sales industry. Today, outside sales professionals who can deliver results are a rare breed and are becoming more and more difficult to find. In fact, talented "inside" salespeople are also hard to find these days.

At age fifty, I decided to reconnect with a friend who owned his own small business. When I mentioned what I was working on, he suggested I focus on small- and medium-sized businesses. "They could really benefit from your creative sales approach," he said.

I did a little research and, sure enough, most people doing what I was considering doing were targeting the big corporations, the big gigs, the big payday. They were taking the same old tired sales crap, repackaging it into some New Age mumbo-jumbo theory, and selling it. And people were buying this crap? Including large corporations?

Taking the road less traveled, while an overused cliché, really made sense to me. I could help, I could lead, and I could measure the results so I would know if my approach really helped. And best of all, I would look like a freaking genius! Or to use a line from the movie *Ever After*, "I will go down in history as the man who opened a door."

Working with small and medium sized businesses makes it easier to measure the results. In large companies and corporations, mid-level and senior management have become masters of coming up with excuses when confronted with poor results: the economy, lazy salespeople, government policies, taxes, poor advertising, etc. In a small business, it is pretty hard to blame someone else.

Early in my consulting career, I was working with my first customer, Mr. Robert Landis. He agreed to be my first client and let me test my approach and process on him—a brave man. In the very first meeting, he was taking notes and kept saying, "This is good stuff," "That is brilliant," and "This is exactly what I need." I was flattered, but I really did not give it much thought. I was just glad he was finding value in our conversations. Then I noticed that this situation kept recurring with our successive meetings.

I realized what I do every day, without even thinking about it, was solid gold to him. I realized what I do day in and day out is valuable and needed by many. What struck me the most was that I came from a printing background, but I was helping someone in the solar/environmental industry, and it really did not matter at all. Everything I do and everything I have done works well in any industry—sales is sales.

So why did I write this book?

First, I believe entrepreneurs and business owners are experts when it comes to their products. They understand a great many things about business, but very few, and I mean very few, are really trained as sales professionals. Consequently, when it comes time to grow their businesses or train someone to sell so they can run their businesses, they get stuck.

I believe:

- **Anyone can sell and everyone should sell.** There is a myth that to be a successful actor or actress one must be good looking. If that were true, then 80 percent of character actors acting today would be out of a job. Like acting, the stereotype that a salesperson must be slick, good looking, a master manipulator, and a smooth talker just isn't true. In fact, in my experience, it's just the opposite. If you can sell a furnace to someone living in the desert, or ice to someone living in the Arctic, you are not a salesperson, you are a con artist. It is my firm belief that with proper training and desire, anyone can be effective in sales.

- **Sales are important.** Every business must have sales to survive. Sales and revenue are not the same thing. Sales can generate revenue, but revenue cannot generate sales. Sales revenue is part of total revenue. If you look up common problems for startups and small businesses, you will find lack of demand, poor cash flow, and lack of access to capital are consistently in the top ten. While not all problems can be solved by increasing sales revenue, nearly every business problem you can think of related to growth can be fixed, or the pain substantially reduced, by increasing revenue through growing sales.

- **New business sales are imperative.** While sales are important, "new business" sales are what this book is really about. Adding new customers and replacing old customers who stop buying from you are the only effective ways to protect and grow your business. Finding new customers is the key to success.

- **Leadership is critical.** I have worked for some great leaders. Conversely, I have worked for some real dolts. A company must have true leadership. Leadership is selling and selling requires leadership. You must lead your company, you must lead your employees, and you must help your customers to see their problems clearly from all angles, then lead the customers in the direction that solves these problems. Regardless of rank, anyone who can sell can lead—it is difficult not to.

- **Sales B.S. is not needed.** Today, there is more sales B.S. in the market than ever before. Just like the myriad of diets that prey on our need to be thin, there are equally as many sales techniques and programs that prey on business owners and promise results. Don't misunderstand me; when it comes to sales, there is a lot of information and many good books that can be very helpful and will teach you a lot; just don't fall for a particular selling strategy as the only strategy. Often, the combination of many approaches tailored to your style will be the most beneficial. However, some of today's sales consultants and gurus are modern-day snake oil peddlers. Many are saying the exact same thing with a different spin or fancy arcane process that only they possess. This is great if you are talking to large corporations that believe throwing money at a problem will fix it. But if you want real results, you must get away from the noise and embrace the basics of selling. The selling formula is quite simple:

  - Have a clearly defined product.
  - Identify your market.

- Have a well thought-out plan.
- Develop a list of potential new customers.
- Get in contact with the right people at the right level within the target company.
- Understand your new prospect's business—clearly identify needs, pain, goals, and objectives.
- Provide a solution that is mapped to the needs, goals, pain, and objectives.
- Gain agreement and move forward.
- Lather. Rinse. Repeat.

Who Will Benefit From This Book?

Have you ever been on a plane and seen that frantic customer running up the aisle because he just realized he was on the wrong plane? I have seen this a few times, and to this day, I wonder how someone can get on a plane bound for Hawaii when he is trying to get to New Jersey. So I think now would be a great time to take a few minutes to ensure that you, the reader, and me, the author, are clear on who this book will serve well.

This book *is* designed for:

1. Entrepreneurs looking to build a company with a strong sales focus. Entrepreneurs who understand that doing this in their business early on has long-lasting benefits. Entrepreneurs who know their product lends itself to human selling—not simply internet-based exchanges.
2. Hobby and farmers market merchants who convert their hobbies into full time businesses and are looking to grow their sales.
3. Micro and small businesses where the owner is currently handling everything, including sales, but in order to grow, needs real sales skills or to train someone to sell so he or she can run the business.
4. Small- and medium-sized businesses that may have no sales force but needs one.
5. Any small- to medium-sized business that is well under capacity

and looking to grow sales to fill this unused capacity.

6. Franchisees who feel the sales approach supplied by the franchisor is either inadequate, not meeting their needs, or missing altogether.
7. NGOs and other organizations that focus on economic development and microenterprises with a focus on business ownership as a way to alleviate poverty both domestically and abroad.
8. Anyone complaining about lack of demand due to government regulations, politicians, crushing taxes, healthcare costs, or the $15 an hour minimum wage—what I like to call "candy-ass excuses." Remember, new business sales can cure nearly every business problem, or at the very least, make problems much less painful.

This book is not designed for:

1. Companies with an existing sales force that isn't performing.
2. Companies looking to train existing salespeople or an existing salesforce.
3. Small business owners who are looking to hire me to sell for them.

Terminology and Definitions

When attempting to simplify any complex process, it's important to establish some basic terminology and definitions to ensure we are all on the same page. Below is a list of words you will read in this book. There is also a list of words that over the years have really pissed me off, and you will not find in this book. (Note: If you do find them in my book, it is because I am using them to illustrate what *not* to say.)

Words/phrases you will hear in my book:

Product	What is your physically deliverable, product, service? I don't separate products/services.
Demand Generation	Create demand for your product or service with sales.

Customer Experience	Will your customer say good things? Bad things? Nothing?
Value Proposition	What value do you provide your customers?
Relevance	Does it really matter, resonate with, or help your customer?
Gain Agreement	What others call closing the sale.
User-Friendly	Is it intuitive, simple, and easy to understand?
Identifying Needs	Understanding what your customer really needs vs. wants.
Identifying Pain	What business problems need to be solved?
Understanding Goals	Where is your customer trying to go?
Clear Objectives	Why are customers trying to get from A to B?
Solution Selling	Understanding business drivers and what problems are tied to them.
Program Solutions	Solutions that have ongoing/lasting positive results and benefits.
Shared Vision	Your ability to tell a story, paint a picture of a journey, share with others, and get buy-in to this vision.
Leadership	This can be anyone in a company. Lead or get out of the way.
Measurable ROI	Is it working? Is it worth it?
Empathy	Feeling another's joy, pain, frustration.

Face to Face	In person.
Sales Cycle	The process from identification to a new happy customer.
Win-Win Outcomes	Customer wins first; you win second.
Teacher	Education is a lot of what a sales professional does.
Consultative Approach	Talk with your customer, not at your customer, and get your customer talking.
Business Drivers	Whatever drives business for each company.
Getting In	You must find a way in, a way to penetrate the company.
Good Questions	Not all questions are equal.
Listening Skills	The ability to really hear and understand what your customer is saying.
Taking Good Notes	You must take notes, period.
Creative Selling	The process of developing your own sales style that works for you.

Words/Phrases you will not hear in my book:

Belly-to-Belly	Gross. How about face-to-face?
Shareholder Value	Not my concern, customers and employees first.
ABC (Always Be Closing)	Just stupid.
People don't want to be sold; they want to buy.	Just very stupid.

People like to be closed.	Are you kidding?
Dial for Dollars	Inefficient, expensive, and trivializes true outreach.
Bid	Don't give your customers any ideas.
Customer Centric	Too buzz-wordy.
Closing the Sale	Sounds negative. How about gaining agreement?
Hook	Assumes customers are suckers or fish.
Cold Calling	I prefer demand generation, business development, or outreach.
Low Hanging Fruit	Does not really exist.
Press Flesh	Just as gross as belly to belly. Just shake hands.

Keep in mind, the words I don't use in my book are not bad. I simply think words are powerful, and in sales, you always need to lead with the positive, not the negative. Selling requires a positive mental attitude, so I find it helpful just to talk in a plain, simple way about what you are doing.

Now that we're on the same page, it's time to begin. Are you ready to grow your small business? Are you ready to figure out how to increase your sales while still keeping your customers happy and coming back for more? Are you ready to live the life you dreamed about when you started your business?

Great. Then you've come to the right place. Let's get started!

Greg W. Anderson

INTRODUCTION
THE SMALL BUSINESS DILEMMA

The following are just a few statistics to highlight the current state of affairs for the small business.

Small Business Statistics

- There are approximately 28 million small businesses in the United States.
- Nearly 21 million are non-employers or do not have additional employees.
- 70 percent of new businesses survive past two years, 50 percent survive past five years, 30 percent survive past ten years, and 25 percent survive fifteen years or longer.
- Of the many reasons why businesses fail, research shows that lack of demand, lack of sales, lack of revenue, and/or lack of new customers are always in the top five.

Now let's look at the small business owners' dilemma.

Sell or Manage?

- Most business owners are not trained in sales.
- Most business owners have a choice—sell for the business or run the business.
- Many owners are deathly afraid of sales.
- Owners not trained in sales make lousy sales trainers.

Here is a true story illustrating the dilemma small businesses face every day.

In the small town of Orting, Washington, is a small residential home building business. It's your typical construction company operated by a husband and wife team, plus their construction supervisor and receptionist. When I first met the owners, business was so good they were building one or two houses at a time and had other excited customers waiting in line. Demand was so good that the owners decided only to build locally, so they actually turned down opportunities from potential customers outside their immediate area.

One night, when I was having dinner with the owners, I asked, "How do you sell your homes?" It was a simple question really, but I was curious about what the sales process looked like in a company with three primary employees and a subcontracted crew.

"Well," the husband replied, "I am the one who does the bids. I am the one who ultimately deals with the incoming calls and meets with potential clients."

"Do you have a sales background?" I asked.

"No, but I really don't need to sell. I have customers calling me looking for my services," he proclaimed.

"Okay. But how do you find customers?" I asked.

Again he said, "The customers find me through word of mouth

and a few well-placed ads."

This response seemed odd to me, but who was I to argue? I was in sales in the printing industry, and he was in the construction industry, yet his answers sort of gnawed at me. I kept thinking his company seemed like it was in a risky situation. But again, who was I to question? He was a successful business owner, and I had never owned a business. He had the nice house with a view, a second retirement home overlooking the water, a new convertible for the weekends parked in the garage, vacations every year, money and wine flowing, and all was good. And I am pretty sure at that time he was making a lot more money than I was. I remember thinking I was missing out. Why didn't I own my own business?

While I am happy to report that today, this company is still building homes, there was a time when business was not as good.

That dinner took place around 2007. As we all know, in 2008, the US economy did a pretty big nosedive that affected many businesses nationwide. As you may also remember, it hit new home construction very hard. The housing market collapsed, and people walked away from homes everywhere. This crisis resulted in a flood of homes on the market and caused the prices of existing homes to fall to a point where one could get a pretty nice house at a price that was better than building one.

As the owner was finishing up the last two houses he was building, he was getting a little uncomfortable because the line of potential customers was not just smaller—it was gone. All the potential customers the company had turned down because they were too far away were looking pretty attractive, but they had either already moved forward with other builders or put home-building plans on hold until the economy improved.

Like every other business, it was time to cut back. The first to go was the receptionist. A once-required position was now an expensive luxury. The next position cut was the construction supervisor.

With no homes being built, no crews were needed, so there was no need for a supervisor. The owners took over these roles. The next victim was the beautiful convertible in the garage. And finally, and probably the most painful, the nearly finished retirement home had to go. However, even after cutting all these costs, there was still no money coming in, so these cuts were simply buying time until the economy improved. It would be a long wait.

I think by now you get the picture. It was a painful situation all the way around, and I am sorry to say there were many more of these stories all across the United States.

Why did this happen? Could anything have been done to prevent it? Sure, a crystal ball would have been nice, but those are in short supply. No one can stop the economy from doing what it will do, but is it possible to be prepared for such a situation and survive? The answer is yes. Many businesses were hurt, but not all went out of business.

First, let's look at what went wrong for this company:

- The owners were confusing "sales" with "revenue."
- The owners were not trained in sales and did not have a pipeline of future work in place.
- The owners had one product line, i.e., new construction, no remodels.
- The owners never had a "need" to think about sales since business was good.
- The owners did not see the "risk" based on the assumption that the economy would always be good.
- The owners did not have or know how to build a sales process into the business.
- By the time the owner felt enough pain to try to solve the problem, there was not enough time to "build" a sales pipeline to solve it.

Bottom line, the owners felt the good times and the demand would always be there, and if "sales" came in by themselves, why go look for customers?

This situation illustrates the biggest small business dilemma: The owner is an expert and understands his or her "business," but the owner is not trained to sell. How should this situation be resolved?

- Should the owner run the business and try to sell?
- Should the owner try to sell? Then who will run the business?
- Should the owner concentrate on running the business and hire someone to sell? This is an expensive option.
- If the owner does have a sales background, who will run the business while he/she is selling?

You can see the dilemma. Is there a solution? Yes, revenue growth through new customer acquisition.

I have spent over a year researching the top "candy-ass" reasons and excuses for why businesses have problems and why many fail. To save you time, I will only list the top ten. They are compiled from many different sources and seem to be recurring issues across many different industries.

Top Ten Problems:
1. Tax rates too high
2. The economy is bad
3. Lack of demand
4. Lack of knowledge/skills
5. Keeping up with technology
6. Healthcare costs
7. Lack of innovation
8. Working capital
9. Getting clients
10. Poor marketing

Note: Not listed and my favorite of all reasons businesses get into trouble or fail: Republicans or Democrats. While both share the blame, the political climate did not consistently fall in the top ten, but I wanted you to understand why I used the term "candy-ass" excuses above.

Did I miss any? Do any of these sound familiar? If so, this book is for you. By the end of the book, you will understand how these issues, and many more, can be removed or substantially minimized as a real problem.

Hopefully, you will come to understand that revenue growth from new business is the Holy Grail for every business. Let me be clear; while revenue growth may or may not fix every problem, it does remove pressure, reduce pain, and allow you more time to understand your problems clearly and find the best creative solution.

"New business revenue growth is the best medicine for most problems faced by startup, small-, and medium-sized businesses."

Many of these top ten issues are faced by corporations as well. But as you might have seen on the news, when there are revenue shortfalls, two things tend to happen. One is very private and one very public. 1) Private: Every salesperson and sales manager in the corporation gets his or her ass kicked to improve sales and meet quotas. 2) Public: Cost cuts. When you hear one-, two- or ten-thousand people are being laid off, it's a response to missing revenue and profit targets. This is the corporate way of keeping the balance between costs and revenue. This is very public. While cost-cutting keeps the accountants and shareholders happy, it's a temporary solution to appease Wall Street. As you may know, small businesses like yours often do not have this lazy option at their disposal. You must have a plan. So let's get started on your plan.

SECTION 1
PRE-SALES PLANNING

Before you can begin building your sales-driven company, you must have a plan. Creating a sales environment is not difficult, but takes some careful and critical thinking to ensure positive results. This foundation must be solid. The following three chapters are an overview that assumes, as a startup or existing business, you have already put a great deal of thought into the following subjects and have a plan for moving forward. Because this book is designed to help you generate revenue by creating sales, I will only go into enough detail to remind you or prod you to build a solid foundation prior to applying the sales strategies we will cover in Chapters 4-10.

Section 1 Highlights

1. What is your product? (Identify/define your product.)
2. What is your value proposition?
3. What is your Unique Selling Proposition (USP)?
4. What problem does your product solve?
5. What is your Go-To-Market strategy (GTM)?
6. How do you create a sales environment?

CHAPTER 1

DO YOU HAVE A PRODUCT?

What Is Your Product?

Many people think this is a trick question. It is not. When talking with small business owners, this is my favorite questions to ask. It is a simple question that usually generates a simple answer but not always the correct answer.

Whether you are providing a tangible item or a service, your product is what your customers are buying from you. It is easy to get caught up in the features and ignore the benefits when trying to figure out what your product actually is. For example, after twenty-eight years in the printing industry, if you asked me what my product is, I would have said I help clients make better business decisions with their marketing communications materials. Of course, I could simply say I sell printing or printing services. In my opinion, that tends to cheapen the work I do. Think carefully about what you sell and how you communicate it to your customers and potential customers. Words are powerful.

Many years ago, I was looking to buy a car. I went to the local car dealership in Tacoma, Washington, where I came across an old high school buddy, Bill. We exchanged a few laughs, and then I asked him, "So what do you do here?" "I sell cars!" he exclaimed. I said, "Great, I'm looking to buy a car," and off we went. He showed me many cool cars in various colors. Some new, some used—oops! I mean pre-owned. I really did not see much I liked. He tried to get me to test-drive a Nissan, but just as I was looking for a way to say no, my wife called, and thankfully, I had my excuse. I told Bill I had to run, but I would be back to continue the search. I took his card, and he took my phone number so we could reconnect. Honestly, I had felt our interaction was a little odd, but I could not put my finger on why.

Fast forward a few days. I was heading home when I happened to pass another car dealership and decided to stop in. After a little browsing, I was approached by a nice guy I'll call Mike. Keep in mind, I did not know Mike and, like every other consumer, my guard was up to protect myself from the dreaded car salesperson. Mike started off with some pleasant small talk, and then he began asking me a few questions. "So," Mike asked, "what are you looking for?" I told him I was looking for a four-door sedan with automatic transmission, a little cool, but not too flashy—and one that got good gas mileage. Mike then asked me *why* these attributes were important to me. I told him I was in sales and often had to drive around with customers, so four doors was much easier, and gas mileage was a no-brainer since I put nearly 100-150 miles a day on my car. Also, I like nice cars, but a flashy car could send the wrong message to my customers. Once at an industry event, a sales guy pulled up in a brand new Mercedes, I had heard a customer say, "Now I know why prices went up last month."

Mike proceeded to ask me a series of questions as we walked and talked. Keep in mind, he had not yet tried to show me a car. After some time and a good conversation, we began looking at the BMW

5 Series, pre-owned. While I liked the 5 Series, Mike informed me that the sporty 328i was not as flashy, had better gas mileage, and was less expensive. Yes, I ended up buying a 328i in green with a tan interior. After all the back and forth and contract signing, I had my new keys and was ready to roll. But I had to ask Mike a question: "Mike, how long have you been selling cars?" His reply has always stuck with me: "*I don't sell cars. I make dreams come true.*"

Mike was a gifted salesperson. In short, he did not try to sell me anything and everything; instead, he tried to understand my needs and provide the best solution for those needs. But most of all Mike taught me that how we talk about what we do or about our product is everything. One guy was selling cars, while the other was making dreams come true. Whom would you rather work with?

So how do you talk about your business or your product to sound more like Mike? I have a favorite process I use for helping customers find the right words. It call it Brand Deconstruction.

Brand Deconstruction is a process I learned at a marketing seminar. In my opinion, before you can talk about your product, you have to develop a way to talk about it. It is important to use specific words that will represent your brand. For example, "Just do it" for Nike and "It gives you wings" for Red Bull energy drinks really tell you nothing about the physical products, but the companies chose those words for a reason. If you brainstormed the meanings and associations behind the words Red and Bull separately you might come up with the following words:

RED:

Blood = energy-speed-accelerate-lift-fly...

Hot = danger-risk-cool-exciting...

Fire = warm-Sun-hot-danger-exciting...

BULL:

Horns = danger-risk-rush-excitement-jump-fall-fly...

Animal = wild-fear-aggressive-adrenaline-no fear...

Spain = fighting-winning-free-soaring...

This is just a small example, but if you do a full word association with these two words, it is not hard to understand why Red Bull's slogan was "It gives you wings." Everything in sales needs to be on purpose.

As you can begin to see, this process helps you better understand and craft your story and messaging to form a cohesive narrative regarding what you do, how you do it, and why you do it. If done correctly and shared, this process can create a theme, brand, or culture around your product, your company, and your mission. Whether you are a salesperson talking to a new potential client, the owner of a company talking to a stranger in an elevator, or the owner of a company talking to a bank about a loan, you must be ready at all times when asked, "So, what do you do?" As we saw with the Bill/Mike story, "I sell cars," is probably not the best answer.

The Two-Minute Irresistible Sales Presentation, with a Twist

What do you do when you are in an elevator or at a luncheon and someone asks you what you do? Many call your response the elevator pitch. But, as I have mentioned, being like "everybody" is not always a good idea. I learned a long time ago about a term called the Two-Minute Irresistible Sales Presentation. I like this term, but I've added my own unique flair to it—a twist. Typically, in a Two-Minute Irresistible Sales Presentation, when someone asks you what you do, the clock starts running and you have about two minutes to share with that person what you do and capture his or her interest.

As usual, I put a little spin on this. I call it my "Galactic Two-Minute Irresistible Sales Presentation." Here is how it works. When asked what I do, I go big, galactic, first. Then, when they ask for clarification, I go into my Two-Minute Irresistible Sales Presentation. Let me give you an example: "I make dreams come true." Remember Mike, the car sales professional? When you first meet

Mike, he will tell you this very same thing. If you get a little curious and ask Mike what he means by that, he will go on to explain how Americans love their cars, and while they are important for earning a living, commuting, and getting around, cars are also part of who we are; they are part of our style, they are freedom, and he has the awesome job of helping people find the perfect fit for their lifestyle.

I once asked a friend of mine what he did for a living. His response, "I sell solar products and installations." This is not very galactic in scope. Why not say instead, "I am helping save the planet each and every day"? Then when I asked how, he could say, "I am providing sales and consulting services to commercial and residential customers who are eager to do their part in protecting the environment by harnessing the power of the sun."

I think you can probably see that by answering on a big and broad (macro) level first, and then moving to the details (micro), you spark curiosity and generate a conversation. The person you are talking to is intrigued; he or she is asking you for more information. And, in the sales game, when a customer or prospective customer is asking you for information, that is the home run. It's important to have a dialogue with your clients. It is no longer a good idea to talk at your clients; you must talk with your clients. When clients ask a question or ask for more information, they are open to a dialogue. They are engaged.

Telling a Story

Okay, you now have a product, you have a word jumble from which to choose the best words, and you have your Galactic Two-Minute Irresistible Sales Presentation. Now what? Well, you have all the pieces in place to begin to do what marketers do every day: tell a story.

My dad is a master potter. A fine arts major in college, he spent his entire career teaching high school print shop and pottery classes. I learned a valuable sales lesson from him one day at the farmers market in little old Puyallup, Washington, when I was there with him selling his pottery. Keep in mind, one of my premises in this book is that anyone can sell and everyone should sell. If you met my dad at age seventy-five, you would not peg him as a salesperson by trade. But Gary Andersen is living proof that with a passion and a little practice, anyone can sell. A customer came up to me who was looking to buy a handmade coffee mug. After my clumsy attempt to "sell," the potential customer moved on. Not too long after, other customers were coming into our booth and Dad was selling them one, two, or even three items. Some would even place orders for dish sets. I was scratching my head, trying to figure out what this seventy-five-year-old gray-bearded teacher knew that I didn't know. I was in sales, for heaven's sake, but what he was doing was working, and what I was doing was not.

Being a teacher by trade, my dad didn't just tell me his secret; he had me watch him a bit, and here is what I saw. He was telling a story to each and every customer. He told how he gets up every morning at 5:00 a.m. and prepares the studio with coffee in hand. He described how he stages his clay, and how he sits down at the wheel next to Potter, his six-year-old black lab, and goes to work. He explained how he creates the mug on the wheel, and how he puts the handle on at just the right time so it will stick. He explained how he would bisque-fire, then glaze-fire to get the final product. And, at the very end of his story, he said, "This is so much fun. If I won the lottery tomorrow, I would keep making pots, but I would just give them away for free to everyone." Holy crap, I wanted to buy a pot after watching this!

Everyone who left dad's booth, whether they bought an item or not had a clear vision of Gary Andersen, the little pottery elf working away in a labor of love making beautiful works of art. (And yes, they usually bought from him.)

I, too, learned to tell the "Lakebay Pottery" story that day, and in the days that followed, as I learned to tell the "Gary Andersen" story, my ability to sell improved radically. As you can see, my dad told the artist's story. Unlike my dad, I was not the artist, so I decided to tell the "dad" story. I talked about my dad at every opportunity. The personal connection between me and my father and the admiration I expressed in my story had a very positive effect. Many of my market neighbors even said they loved hearing me talk about him. It really personalized the experience. Honestly, though, I was never as good at telling it as my dad—who could be? He was the original elf!

As you can probably see, it is all about the story. Every product, every company, and every business owner has a story, and a well-crafted story is what you are trying to develop. This story is what provides the customer with not only the product's intrinsic value, but its emotional connection.

What Is Your Value Proposition?

As you have seen, it is important to think critically about what your product is, what words you use to describe it, and the story behind your product or business. The next step in the process is to understand and communicate to your clients and prospective clients the value proposition, or why your product has value and what its benefits are.

If you look up the dictionary definition of a value proposition, it is pretty bland and straightforward. Like everything else, though, I would go a bit further. I see a value proposition as a unique promise to your marketplace—a promise that must be clearly explained and a promise that must be kept at all costs.

Value propositions, by nature, are unique to each company. Your value proposition is what sets you apart from your competition.

Your value proposition should be clear, bold, and intertwined into every part of your business, especially the sales process. It should communicate why your product has value, what the benefits are, and how you deliver it.

Value propositions are basically perceived costs vs. perceived benefits. If the perceived benefits are higher than the perceived costs, customers are more apt to buy from you.

Here are a few questions to answer when thinking about your value proposition:

- What product or service is your company actually selling?
- What is the benefit of using it?
- Who are your target customers for this product/service?
- What makes your product unique and/or different?
- What does your product do that others do not?

There are many resources online for learning how to develop and structure a value proposition. I would suggest you do some simple online searching for information on Value Propositions. There are a lot of excellent sites that show how to create and structure a powerful value proposition.

What Is Your Unique Selling Proposition (USP)?

Simply put, a USP is what you bring to the marketplace that sets you apart from others in your industry. It can be the lowest price, fastest turn-around time, highest quality, etc. All business owners need to figure out what is unique about their business or they run the risk of becoming a "me too" business. A "me too" business is one in which the business offers the same products and services as its competitors and cannot set itself apart. For example, when talking to a customer who says your competition has high quality, you would say, "Me too." When a customer says "Your competition is fast" you would say, "Me too." When a customer says, "Your competition has the latest and greatest widget maker," you would say, "Me too." This situation, where you simply let your customer know you can do everything your competition can do, is not good enough.

You can make your selling proposition unique by figuring out a way to separate yourself from your competition, but this requires a lot of creativity. Let me give you an example.

Back in the 1990s, when I graduated college, I started my career in sales at my first printing company, Valco Graphics. At that time, another printing company was also doing well despite being small and not well located. This company was nothing special, but they had a loyal following, and every time I lost to them, I had to wonder why. One day after losing, again, I had to ask my customer what it is about that company that was so compelling. To my surprise, she said, "They don't charge for overs."

Let me explain "overs." In printing, it's pretty hard to stop a press and bindery equipment at an exact quantity. Most companies shoot for a target quantity. If you have a lot of waste in the process, you might get a few less than you ordered. This is known as "unders." If you did not have much waste, you might get a few extra, known as "overs." You are charged for the overs and you receive a credit for any unders on your invoice. Many customers had a hard time understanding why they couldn't simply order 10,000 and get 10,000. The concept of unders/overs to this day is still a bit challenging for customers.

This company saw the frustration with unders/overs as an opportunity for a unique selling proposition. It decided never to charge for overs, and customers loved that. This company took a pain point and made it disappear; it took a confusing industry process and made it simple; it took an additional cost item and reduced it to "zero." All this company really did was to convert a negative into a positive.

Keep in mind that, like a value proposition, a unique selling proposition can be a real or perceived benefit. If the customer perceives the benefit is greater than the cost, then the customer believes he or she is receiving value. In this situation, the printer most likely built in enough waste to never go under and altered its pricing structure so the base cost included any possible overs. But it worked and worked well.

What Problem Does Your Product or Service Solve?

Every company was started for a reason. Every product and/or service fills a need that people are willing to pay to have met. If not, they will go elsewhere to find a solution.

In this day and age, it's important to clearly articulate what your product does, how it does it, and why your product is the best.

Does your product solve a problem? There are many products on the market that people *need*—food, water, shelter, healthcare, transportation, medicine, etc. But there are many, many more products on the market that people *want*.

No one needs a pet rock or a chia pet, but someone is making big bucks off this *want*. Everyone needs food, shelter, and healthcare, so many people are also making big bucks providing solutions for these needs.

Later in this book, you will hear a lot about needs. But, in any case, people have both needs and wants. If your product solves a problem that is a need or a want in any way, it is important that you include that problem and how you product solves it in your value proposition and how you talk to your customers. Start looking for ways your product solves a problem and provides a benefit.

What Is a BATNA?

BATNA stands for "Best Alternative to a Negotiated Agreement."

This term was coined by Roger Fisher and William Ury in their 1981 book, *Getting to Yes*. Simply stated, if I am at a market negotiating with a vendor who wants $50 and I want to pay $40, and I know a comparable product is at another booth for $40, then I have an alternative.

While the term BATNA is most commonly about negotiating, I think the concept can apply to the sales process as well. To make it a little more relevant, I would like to coin my own term. Unfortunately, there is no catchy acronym for "Best Alternative to Not Buying from Me," but I think you get the picture. It is important to ask yourself, "If they don't buy from me, who will they buy from?" There are many reasons customers decide not to buy from you, but for now, let's talk about the competition.

When you started your business, you probably asked yourself a few questions like:

- Is my product truly unique? Am I without competition? (Usually the answer is no.)
- Is my business one of three that can provide this product/service, or is it a crowded field?
- Who is my competition?
- Can I compete with my competition on price, quality, and services?
- Is my product/service superior to the competition?
- Do I have the ability to add new products as needed?

You can probably see where I am going with this. Unless you are selling a product that no one else can supply, you had better have a plan to compete because your customers will have other options. Heck, if you really are the only game in town, one of your customers may just start a business to compete with you.

Summary

As you can see, the question, "What is your product?" is not as easy to answer as one would think. How you talk about your business and the story you tell needs to be yours and yours alone. Similarly, the value you bring, the problem you solve, and why you are the best alternative are all critical elements that enable you to set yourself apart from the competition and create a dialogue with your customer. If done correctly, these attributes become part of your product.

Once you have the answers to these questions, you will be ready to take your product to market and communicate clearly who you are, what you are doing, and why you are doing it in your own unique way.

Now, the question becomes: How do you approach your market, and what tools will you use to execute this approach? The following chapter will talk about developing a go-to-market (GTM) strategy.

Exercise

1. What is your product?

    _____

    _____

    _____

    _____

2. What will you highlight in your Two-Minute Irresistible Sales Pitch?

    _____

    _____

    _____

    _____

3. What is your story?

    _____

    _____

    _____

    _____

4. What is your Value Proposition?

    _____

    _____

    _____

    _____

5. What is your Unique Selling Proposition?

_____

_____

_____

_____

6. What problem does your product or service really solve?

_____

_____

_____

_____

7. If customers don't buy from you, who will they buy from?

_____

_____

_____

_____

CHAPTER 2

DO YOU HAVE A GO-TO-MARKET STRATEGY?

Go-To-Market Strategy (GTM)

Simply put, a GTM is an action plan that lays out how a company will reach its customers. It is also a blueprint for how to provide pricing, products, and services to those customers. Often, it is documented in a business plan. The GTM is a critical part of defining and creating a competitive advantage in your marketplace.

As you can see, a GTM has many facets. Since this book is focused on sales/demand generation, I will focus my comments primarily on the sales side of the GTM. Following are things to take into account when considering your GTM from a sales perspective.

Are You a B2B or B2C?

Two basic types of markets exist: B2B (Business to Business) and B2C (Business to Consumer). If you are a shoe manufacturer selling shoes to retail shoe companies, which then sell shoes to the public, you are in the B2B market. If your business sells shoes to consumers in the mall, you are in the B2C market. If you are a manufacturer who sells shoes to the public via outlet stores and other retailers also carry your shoes, you are in both markets. In this day and age, it can be difficult to be all things to all people, so it is important to figure out what you are and what you want to be.

While it is difficult, it is not impossible for large and small businesses to do both. If you were to walk into any small, local print shop to print a personal project, the print shop would take your money and deliver your product just fine. However, the shop will also work for other small businesses that probably need printing far more often and in greater volume than the average walk-in client. Similarly, large businesses see the value of supporting both B2B and B2C markets. Companies like Cisco have a foot in each market. They have consumer products and enterprise products. One challenge is effectively marketing and selling to each. Cisco's company tagline is "Welcome to the human network." As you can see, it is overly broad, but it does cover both markets. While we live in an age of specialization and focus, I do feel that if you can effectively market to both and support both, you can grow your business and diversify your customer base at the same time. Each market does, however, require a little different approach from a sales and demand generation point of view, so let's briefly look at those approaches.

B2B

B2B businesses are quite different from B2C businesses. If we go back to the shoe manufacturer who sells shoes to retailers, then the need for salespeople becomes more apparent. You now have a situation where one salesperson is selling skids and possibly container loads of shoes to a customer or to multiple customers. In theory, you could have one salesperson handling millions of dollars' worth of orders to one or multiple clients. It is not only imperative that these accounts are well taken care of, but that the salesperson can acquire new accounts to grow the business.

Unlike the B2C model, in the B2B model, the need for a trained sales/demand generation expert is paramount. Salespeople handle incoming sales calls, problem resolution, pricing objections, new product requirements, new product rollouts, and any sales-related issues the customer might have. While this book may appear focused more on B2B businesses, many of the concepts and elements of the sales process are still relevant for B2C businesses.

B2C

B2C businesses are more typically retail establishments. As in our shoe store example, whether you are selling one pair or multiple pairs of shoes to the general public, you still need salespeople to help and assist as customers enter the store. This type of inside sales staff is usually compensated through hourly pay or a combination of hourly and commission. In this situation, you are selling from brick and mortar or online to anyone and everyone who has access to your store(s) and website. Typically, outside salespeople are not common since the focus is selling a product or service to a person, not to an account in bulk. Most person-to-person contact, if part of your GTM, is handled via internet, phone, a trained customer service technician, or call center resource.

Both B2B and B2C

While many feel they have to pick, you can support both consumers (B2C) and businesses (B2B). There are those who say you should pick one and focus, and there are those who say you can expand your business by correctly marketing and advertising to both markets. I would suggest you pick one to start, with the idea that at some point in the future you will add the other.

Inside Sales, Outside Sales, or Both?

Deciding on a model will drive how you develop your sales approach. If you are primarily focusing on the traditional brick-and-mortar B2C strategy, then you will probably be fine with customer service people and internal salespeople.

If you are looking at a hybrid or a B2B focus, you will have to consider whether you are going to look at an inside salesperson or an outside salesperson. The inside salesperson acts more as a customer service/salesperson for inbound calls and requests and really does not leave the office. This scenario requires you to have advertising or a lead-generation strategy that drives potential customers to your business.

The outside salesperson allows you to break your customer service and sales into two different departments. The reason you want this division is because when salespeople are out doing their jobs and they bring in opportunities, someone needs to process the orders internally, so the salespeople can go back out and keep selling.

In my opinion, companies have three options when looking to create an outside sales team: 1) You can partner with people who do not work for you and pay them a small commission or finder's fee if they send work your way. 2) You can start off with one person in-house as a customer service/salesperson. As soon as business and revenues start to grow, an opportunity may arise to convert this in-house person into an outside salesperson. While the person is inside, he or she can still develop the skills necessary to be successful selling outside. 3) To get the process rolling, you can outsource your sales efforts. Since a small business may not want to invest the money and/or time, it may wish to have a contractor handle all or part of the sales process. Depending on your business and product/services, outsourcing may be a good way to start.

Sales Channels

How are you going to sell your product? The answer is important because some channels fill the role salespeople might otherwise cover. Following are a few different channels for generating revenue that are often called sales.

Online: While this is a great way to go to market, many mistakenly think all they need to do is create a website and add some search engine keywords, and customers will beat a path to their door. If you have online marketing skills or access to an online marketing expert, this transition can be far easier. Beyond a website, many other ways exist to take part in the online marketplace. For example, Amazon, eBay, ETSY, and many more outlets will, for a fee, allow you to sell through them. This process can be challenging, but rewarding if your product/service is one in which human interaction is not required to complete the sale.

Affiliate Sales: This type of sales works well for both physical human sales and online sales. The idea is similar to outsourcing; you simply pay people a commission or fee for selling your products and/or directing people to your website. If this works well, you receive an additional benefit because now you, the owner, can run the business while there is a mechanism in place to sell.

VAR (Value-Added Resellers): While most common in the tech industry, VAR can also work for other industries. VARs are companies that purchase your products, then add them to a bundle with other products, then resell them to their customers. One advantage to this approach is that you, as a small business, can gain access to a variety of new markets through your VAR and the demand for your products could grow. Of course, though you will never get full retail price when selling in this space, the additional volume can be attractive. Just don't get caught in the "make it up in volume" trap. At some point, you have to charge a fair price to remain profitable.

Distributors: This is a true wholesale arrangement. In this scenario, you rely on distributors with their own salesforces to sell your products. It is critical that your business plan is set up for this arrangement because, like the VAR model, you will have to sell at wholesale rates. Even though using distributors may not require you to hire salespeople, you or someone initially has to reach out and build a distributor network, which requires selling the distributors on your product.

Catalog Sales: Another way to generate sales revenue is to create a catalog and mail it to customers. This requires printing, mailing, and list purchasing, as well as having someone in your office (customer service people) to receive phone calls and process orders. If your catalog can drive customers to your website to place orders, even better. While many businesses are built around one specific sales channel, it is possible to embrace more than one. In my opinion, a diverse set of sales channels is always best when possible.

Social Media: I would be remiss if I did not at least address social media and the roll it can play in facilitating sales for a small business. But, make no mistake, while some direct sales are occurring on some social media platforms, most of the activity in the social media space is geared toward awareness, creating demand, and building an audience. Expecting to sell only through social media channels is probably not the best strategy—yet. I am guessing we are not too far away from a business model that is heavily social-media driven.

Having said that, there are lots of social media tools to choose from and many ways to help grow sales. Whether it is simple or complex, a social media plan can help you create demand that will drive sales. In my honest opinion, the biggest way social media can help is with lead generation and building a market. So, unless you are a social media expert or have a family member who is, here are just a few simple ways to use social media:

- **Facebook:** Making friends on Facebook is a great place to start building your fan base. You can have a personal page and/or a business page to help people find you.

- **LinkedIn:** Network and join LinkedIn groups. Like Facebook, you are looking for visibility and to connect with customers and/ or potential partners. You can also write and submit articles to boost your visibility.

- **YouTube:** Videos are hot and videos sell. They even the playing field for companies unable to afford TV commercials that want to demonstrate a product. There are many young videographers to choose from, and adding a video to your website can be a good way to reach your target market.

- **Twitter:** Twitter has emerged as a way to start conversations, and with hashtags, allows for potential customers to dial into a specific conversation. With some creative, well-thought-out posts, you can start a conversation and drive people to your website.

- **Pinterest:** Pinterest is a great way to show videos, podcasts, and images of your product that will get shared. It's a good way to inspire and connect with potential customers.

- **Tumblr:** Tumblr is a blog-based social media site that allows you to run contests, provide coupons, and stay interesting and relevant to your audience or store.

- **ETSY:** At ETSY, you can actually make direct sales. Small companies like jewelry makers and pottery artists are actively selling products there. ETSY allows you to set up an online mini-store that you can tie in with your marketing efforts and other social media platforms.

- **SnapChat:** SnapChat on average reaches 41 percent of 18-34 year olds daily. That statistic alone is pretty amazing. Like Instagram, it is more of a marketing/targeting or brand-awareness medium and less of a direct sales tool. But marketing and brand awareness usually precede a purchase, so you cannot ignore SnapChat if you are targeting the 18-34-year-old market. Unlike Instagram, SnapChat data does not hang out long and is often referred to as self-destructive data. In other words, the data is not like an email that retains an email train—once sent it is gone. This self-destructive feature can actually build a sense of urgency, which can be good.

- **Instagram:** Many are using Instagram as a marketing tool. Viewers can see your brand or get a behind-the-scenes view of what you and your products are all about. Once you master the hashtag process, you can target your messages and take part in conversations with potential customers. If you are looking to connect with the younger generation or connect globally, it is an excellent platform.

Keep in mind, every one of the social media sites I have mentioned (except ETSY) is designed to drive traffic and start a conversation. So if you don't have a website for your business, you had better get one. If you have a website that is purely informational, it might be a good idea to add an e-commerce button and shopping cart functionality to enable your customers to make an actual purchase. If you are going to use social media to create awareness and drive customer demand, you need a place for your customers to land and possibly buy without your direct involvement.

Make sure you have thought through your plan and tested it. Many people simply create an account at social media sites, and then they sit back and wait for traffic. Social media takes effort and requires fresh, relevant content. Also, make sure your business and product are a good fit for the social media site's audience. Not every product and business will get the same results. You can also employ one or multiple social media platforms; there is no requirement to take part in all of them.

Customer Service and the Customer Experience

If you are working your way toward having a full-time salesperson, you also have to be thinking about a customer service component to your business. Again, regardless of how you go to market and what sales channel you choose to employ, you must have a way to process orders at all times. If you have salespeople, you need to handle incoming orders. If you do not yet have salespeople, then you need a really good customer service person to provide your customers with a good experience.

Never underestimate the weight of a positive or negative customer experience. Your sales infrastructure must not negatively impact your customer. Remember, happy customers may or may not share their experiences with others. But in today's social media age, angry customers will share with anyone and everyone. Make sure you are always on top of the customer experience.

Regardless of which sales channel(s) you elect to use or whether you decide on B2B, B2C, or a hybrid approach, it is a good idea to break the sales side down into two different types. While there are probably more than two, I will focus on the two I feel are most relevant to the small business owner. These are transactional sales and solution/program sales.

Transactional: Transactional sales are fairly straightforward. A customer gives you the specifications for a project; you create a price quote; you build the product, deliver the product, invoice for the product, then get paid for it—end of sale. This may be a one-time sale, or it could be a sale that recurs as the need arises. A transactional sale will always have a start and a stop, like a project.

- **Characteristics:** Short cycle times, defined start and stop dates, can be B2B or B2C, usually involves a buyer and seller only, more job-focused than program-focused.

- **Example:** Car sales, home sales. Once you buy and have finalized the deal, not much is left for the salesperson to do except stay in touch and try to get referrals.

Solution/Program Selling: Solutions sales are far more complex. For example, a customer has a program that is ongoing and has no real stop date because it is part of the customer's daily operation. Again, the customer provides specifications; however, in this case, the specifications are not simple, but complex and affect different parts of your customer's business (technology, accounting, management, HR, etc.). The customer is looking for a program you can build and implement that stays up and running and may also be expanded as needs grow. This is more of a consultative type of selling. The process for understanding your customer's needs and doing a thorough needs analysis is more time-consuming, and the information you need may come from different departments within your customer's business. Also, because your solution is not simply a one-off, but a multi-faceted solution, it must be engineered and tested to ensure all stakeholders' interests are addressed and their needs are met.

- **Characteristics:** Longer sales cycle; detailed needs analysis; can involve many people; can take many days, weeks, or months to implement; ongoing in nature; usually involves senior management approval; is more program-focused than job-focused.

- **Example:** Software sales, security systems sales, outsourcing sales, etc.

With both the transactional and solution sales models, myriad approaches exist. Pick up one of the many sales books on the market and you will see how many different types of selling systems there really are. A selling system, sometimes called a selling methodology, is simply a process you work through to obtain new customers. This book describes my selling system that I am sharing with you. Many sales professionals have some sort of system, whether they have adopted one or they use a hybrid of a few different systems. The key is that you need a method to your approach. In Chapter 7, in the section titled "A Quick Overview of a Few Different Sales Systems," I will provide a list of a few popular selling systems to illustrate how important it is to figure out your style and what will work for you.

Regardless of whether you are a B2B, B2C, or hybrid of both, you will need to identify who your customer is and what he or she looks like.

Who Is Your Target Customer?

Today, it is important to map out and list every possible business that could become your customer. This is known as a lead list in sales, and it helps define your marketplace and provide direction. The last thing you want to do is waste your time talking to the wrong type of customer or trying to get an account, only to find out the customer would never buy your product for some unforeseen reason.

Similarly, if you are developing an advertising or marketing plan for your B2C and B2B market, you will also need to figure out whom to target.

Prioritize Your Target Customers and Prospective Customers

Personally, I divide my lists into A, B, C, and D customers and A, B, and C prospects. Let me explain these designations:

A customers: Existing Big Fish. Massive amounts of revenue. Caring for one single big fish could be all you do. A customers tend to be more contractual in nature. Protect these customers at all costs.

A prospects: Every salesperson must have a few A prospects in the portfolio and a few being worked on at all times. A prospect can take months or years to land, but it is worth it.

B customers: Existing Medium Fish. These tend to be the bulk of your sales portfolio, generating less revenue, but they are very active and require your attention. These customers can tend to come and go more frequently than the Big Fish. They provide you with good revenue, but you could not make a living on one account. These customers tend to be more transactional and can require more time to manage.

B potential prospects: Anyone who could become a B or A customer in time is a good B potential customer. Some are and will always be B customers, and that's okay. You need lots of them. B customers have a stabilizing effect on your business. If one B customer or a dozen leave, you still have your Big Fish and can recover. If one Big Fish leaves, you may still be okay if you have a diverse mix of B customers.

C customers: Small existing customers who could become A or B clients in time. You may be only handling a few projects here and there; they do have potential, but currently are only producing small amounts of revenue.

C prospects: Small leads that could climb to C customers. This is where you have to start valuing your time. Time spent on a C prospect or customer who does not have a very good chance of becoming an A or B customer is dangerous. Sure, when you are new or revenues are down, you scramble and fight for everything. But at some point, you must recognize when the cost of dealing with a C customer or prospect is simply too great and can start slowing your growth.

D customers/prospects: These are very small customers who really can't become an A or B or even a C customer and do not currently generate any revenue. These tend to be referrals, or call-ins on the phone or internet. It is important to qualify and only pursue the ones that have a chance of success. It is always good to have a referral network at your fingertips. I find when I refer clients away, two things happen: 1) Customers thank me for being so helpful and honest about not being the best resource for them, and 2) The person or company I refer them to usually calls to thank me. And when that person or company has a referral that is not a good fit, it is sent my way. Win-win!

Where Do Your Prospects Live?

Most products today are not designed to fit or attract everyone. Also, competition exists since you are probably not the only one providing your product or service.

In the printing industry, there are two types of customer: end-users and agencies. End-users are like Microsoft. They need printing, so they go out and buy printing from a vendor base. Agencies are design, creative, and/or advertising firms. They manage and source the printing for their clients.

Both are good, but different. I have had end-users who generated $2 million in revenues, and I have worked with agencies that only generate $50,000. I have also had end-users who spend $50,000 and agencies that send work worth millions of dollars my way.

You can *spend* your time working on one end-user account, and if you win, you win one account. Or you can *spend* your time working on one agency account, and when you are successful, you may support ten or twenty different accounts. The operative word here is "spend." You must spend your time wisely in order to get the best return on investment for every hour spent in the sales role.

So where do your customers live? Where can you find multiple customers in one spot? Trade shows, associations, seminars, events, fairs, PTA, clubs…? The list is endless.

It is sort of like panning for gold versus mining for gold.

In my limited experience panning for gold, I found a nugget here and a nugget there, which can make for a long day. But when it comes to mining for gold, once you find a vein, keep mining that vein.

How Will You Contact Your Potential Customers?

Once you have found potential customers, what is your approach for contacting them: phone, fax, email, direct mail, snail mail, letter, FedEx, carrier pigeon? Assuming you or your salespeople will reach out, what will you say to a potential new customer?

As you can probably tell, here is where the rubber meets the road. Here is where your product, your value proposition, your unique selling proposition, and your story all come together and paint a picture of what your company does, how it does it, and why it does it.

I will go into this much further in the last seven chapters of this book, but before you can begin to contact and bring in new customers, you must first create a sales environment. You must have a sales-driven mentality that puts the customer's needs front and center. You must have a process that you or your sales team can use that is intuitive, easy to duplicate, and easy to teach to all new salespeople at your company. As a business owner, you must create a sales environment before you can really build the sales organization.

Summary

Before you can take your product to market, you need to have a plan and a strategy that fits your business. Understanding who you are and what markets you plan to serve is critical when it comes to creating the infrastructure to support you efforts. You must be clear on what sales channels you will use and what type of customer service solution you will put in place in order to define, find, target, and prioritize the types of customers you seek. In the following chapter, we will explore how to create the sales environment you will need to succeed.

Exercise

1. What is/are your go-to-market strategy/strategies?

   _____

   _____

   _____

   _____

2. Are you going to serve the B2B or B2C market or both?

   _____

   _____

   _____

   _____

3. Will you use inside or outside salespeople?

   _____

   _____

   _____

   _____

4. What sales channels fit your company best?

   _____

   _____

   _____

   _____

5. How will you handle customer service?

_____

_____

_____

_____

6. Who is your target customer?

_____

_____

_____

_____

7. Where does your target customer live?

_____

_____

_____

_____

8. How will you contact you target customer?

_____

_____

_____

_____

CHAPTER 3

CREATING A SALES ENVIRONMENT

What does the proper sales foundation look like?

Not too long ago, I was working with a contractor who was representing a firm with about $7 million in annual revenue. This firm had been successful for the past ten years and had rapidly grown to the $7 million mark by just keeping up with orders as they came in.

At this company, there were no salespeople. If you called the company, you would be connected to one of two technical people who would proceed to walk through a five-page technical document to gather the necessary data. If all the questions could not be answered, there would have to be a second call. Once the questionnaire was filled out, this internal technical person would have the company VP build a proposal from a template, with pricing included. The technician would then email the "bid" to the customer and await the response.

This process had worked for many years based on this unique industry experiencing some rapid growth. At first, there were few product/service providers in the industry, but more and more players were entering the market. Sales had begun to flatten, and since the government incentives could expire in the near future, the owners were getting a little concerned that the $7 million in revenue could start shrinking. Heck, if revenues simply remained at $7 million, it would mean the company was falling behind.

Business is always good *until* it is not. Selling or creating demand is not needed *until* it is needed.

Many companies find themselves in this predicament. The time to create a sales-driven organization is when things are good, not after they turn bad. When times are good, you have money and resources and can build a well-thought-out sales plan. In times of crisis, money and resources are scarce and with the learning curve involved, you may not fix the revenue shortfalls in time to avert disaster.

Whether you, as the owner, are going to start selling or are looking to bring on a sales professional, the following is a to-do list of items that must be understood and in place before you can evolve from a passive sales organization to an action-oriented sales organization. You must create a sales environment. You can do this by:

1. Understanding the difference between sales and revenue
2. Understanding what a "sales environment" is
3. Knowing how your customers do or will buy from you?
4. Putting the right tools in place
5. Making proper use of technology
6. Envisioning your selling workflow/process
7. Creating a compensation plan
8. Knowing how you will handle customer service
9. Creating a sales-driven culture
10. Providing effective leadership

For the remainder of this chapter, we'll look at each one of these items.

Understanding the Difference Between Sales and Revenue

First, let's define what sales are and how they are different from revenue. While you might see this as splitting hairs, the difference is important. Not all sources of revenue are equally reliable, predictable, or repeatable.

- **Revenue:** Revenue is all the money brought into a company through various streams.
  - Sales, lease payments, interest payments, royalties, donations, etc.
- **Sales:** Sales is merely one of the revenue streams listed above or the amount your customers pay for your product and/or service.

For most businesses, generally speaking, sales is the largest component or the dominant revenue stream for a company. That is why many think of sales and revenue as the same thing.

Since you are this far into this book, I will share with you how I view sales. To me, there are two types of sales: sales from existing customers and new business sales. While both are important, my primary focus has always been on new business sales, since it is the lifeblood for growing any company. To me, sales are defined as "What revenue you bring in on purpose." If you have a plan and a process, and as a result, you "bring in" business, this is sales. Here are the reasons I define sales in this way:

1. **Controlling your own destiny:** If you have a plan and a process and it brings in business, you can measure the results and improve the numbers if you wish. To grow a business, you must have a process in place that is consistent, measurable, and repeatable.

2. **Luck:** Movie Director James Cameron and author Rick Page have both used the phrase, "Hope is not a strategy." If a customer finds you and "happens" to spend money, great, take it. To me this is not "on purpose." This is not predictable or

measurable, and it is not a strategy for long-term success. Sales must be "on purpose."

3. **The Pareto Principle (80/20 rule):** As you know, 20 percent of your customers usually make up 80 percent of your revenue. Similarly, in every industry, a percentage of your customers will die, move away, change vendors, or get bought by a larger corporation, and all of these can affect your business. If you get too comfortable with simple walk-in sales and your existing customers, you are simply setting a trap for yourself. What if one of your customers decides to leave and they also happen to be in the top 20 percent of your revenue bucket? Or, worse yet, what if it is one of your top three customers? If this happens, you can be in real trouble overnight.

As you can see, sales from existing customers and creating new business sales are critical if you want to protect and grow your current business. To do this, you will need to create a "sales environment" within your own company. And yes, you can create a sales environment and sales process even if you are a company of one, two, or three people.

Understanding What a "Sales Environment" Is

Imagine if you worked in the commercial real estate industry. Think about what a real estate agent needs to hit the pavement or get on the phone and generate business. If the agent is good at her job and begins interacting with customers, what would she need from you to create a customer and begin generating revenue? How long would it take to start generating revenue? I would say the company with the sales infrastructure and an established sales environment will get there faster. It is critical that you and your team start making decisions always with the following question in mind: "Will this help grow sales?" A sales environment is as much an attitude as a process.

While you can roll out your sales process all at once, smaller businesses looking to start off the process can begin slowly. If you are just starting, I recommend creating an outline that lists the steps you visualize will be necessary to get your company where you need it to be. Then, you can slowly roll out what you need, when you need it. The following section will go into a little detail on what you may want to consider in your plan.

Knowing How Your Customers Buy or Will Buy from You

Do you know how your customers buy or will buy from you? This may seem like an odd question, but I assure you it is not. If a customer is confused about how to buy or finalize a transaction, that customer will buy from someone else or delay. A clear, concise process needs to exist for buying your product or service.

Here is an example of the process of buying in the printing industry.

1. Customer sends a printing company a set of specifications for a new project.

2. Printing company provides a written proposal (hopefully, in person) with all terms and conditions spelled out.

3. Printing company provides samples and other customer testimonials/references of happy customers for whom it produced similar work.

4. Customer signs and dates the quote letter specifying the quantity and delivery details and this becomes the contract.

5. Customer sends purchase order to the printing company if a purchase order system is used. If not, the signed proposal is the contract.

6. Printing company sends the customer a credit application so it can choose to pay through COD, a credit card, or by opening a Net 30 account.

7. Printing company processes the application and sets up the account.

8. Printing company provides a schedule for when graphic files need to be in to hit the customer's target date.

9. Graphic files arrive and off they go.

Obviously, buying printing from a printer is a fairly straightforward process. Your business may be more or less complex, but the bottom line is to make it easy and simple to buy from you.

Putting the Right Tools in Place

Internally, some basic tools must be in place before you can really hit the ground running in sales.

1. Computer

2. Research tools (Hoovers, Reference USA Database, etc.) These tools are explained in Chapter 4.

3. Online or physical contracts and legal paperwork if needed

4. Proposal templates

5. Estimate request templates

6. Estimate input templates

7. Customer relationship management (CRM) database for managing your current customers and keeping track of progress on all prospects. You can start off using Excel, but eventually, a CRM system will make more sense.

8. Net 30 credit application process, cash, credit, credit card, etc.

9. Sales literature, presentation folders, letterhead, business cards

10. Samples, if applicable

11. Customer testimonials/references

12. Sales training manual for all new hires to ensure all are working

from the same playbook

13. Website

Before you can sell or have a sales professional hit the street, you must have the basic tools in place.

Making Proper Use of Technology

In this day and age, not every small business is able to employ all the latest and greatest technology, but you can do some things for a nominal expense that will pay dividends now and in the future.

Of course, I am assuming all business owners understand the value of having computers, mobile devices, offsite storage, and backup services in place. The following is a quick list of the different types of technologies being used by small businesses today in the sales and marketing space:

- **Email Marketing:** Infusionsoft, Hubspot, Constant Contact, Mail Chimp

- **Planning and Organizing Tools:** Evernote, Trello, Slack

- **File Transfers Tools:** Dropbox, Google Drive, Hightail, Ter-ashare, WeTransfer, Send Space, DropSend

- **Social Network Tools:** LinkedIn, Pinterest, Facebook, Twitter, Instagram

While there are a variety of business software and technology tools on the market for accounting, human resources, manufacturing, and Management Reporting Systems (MRP), for the purposes of our discussion, I will focus on sales-related technology tools. To that end, I will spend most of my time talking about Customer Relationship Management (CRM) solutions.

Keeping track of sales data is critical for all businesses, with certain sales metrics being the foundation of a sales plan that looks for growth and improvement every year. The best way to keep track of sales data is through a CRM system. Ideally, if you have a CRM system that links to an MRP system, all your data will reside in one database. This is quite expensive, so a stand-alone CRM system will suffice for a small business.

A variety of CRM systems are on the market, ranging from free to massively expensive, so a little research in this area is needed to ensure you know what you do and do not need. This is not one of those situations where the more you spend for bells and whistles, the better off you are. In all reality, you may not need many bells or whistles to get a good return.

Following is a brief list of some CRM systems with a few notes. Please investigate what fits your business best.

Startup:

- **Hubspot:** Hubspot is a free CRM system for all users. It has premium features and online support.

Free:

- **Zoho:** Zoho is a CRM system that is free for up to ten users. It includes premium features and help desk and online support forums.

Very Small Business:

- **Insightly:** Insightly is a CRM system that is free for up to two users. It currently charges $12/month for each additional user. It is scalable to help as your business grows, and it has phone, email, and help desk support.

Small Business:

- **Salesforce:** Salesforce is a CRM system that currently charges

$25/user per month. It is probably the most popular and versatile CRM system on the market with 24/7 home and live chat support.

Note: These are just a few of many CRM tools on the market. Additional CRM software solutions and other tech tools are listed at the end of this book.

You will see that as you dig into this, for a nominal fee, or even free, you have access to quite a variety of CRM solutions and features that can help track and grow sales now and in the future. One key to success with any CRM system is that whoever is using it must enter data every day. If you try to backfill the data from your notes at the end of the week, a CRM system is not going to help. You will forget details if you do this.

Also, if you have team members who will be using this CRM system, it is critical that you show them its value and how it can help them. In my experience, when owners or senior management require their teams to use a CRM system, it is viewed more as a big brother is always watching thing than as a sales tool. Sure, a CRM makes it easier to monitor sales activity, but that is not a negative and must be portrayed in a positive light for all to adopt the tools.

What type of sales metrics do we want to collect and why? Below is a quick overview of what is important to track.

1. **What prospects does the company have?** Keeping track of all your prospects is critical, especially as you start to grow your business and add new contacts.

2. **In what industries are these prospects?** With all your prospects in one database, you can now sort by tagging each with an industry code, and you can start to see a picture of where you are having the most success.

3. **In what part of the sales cycle are these prospects?** When you start having sales success, it is important to know where each prospect is in the sales cycle. It is also good to know, for exam-

ple, if you have all your prospects in the final stages and none in the beginning stages; then it's time to feed the pipeline.

4. **How many estimates are generated?** If you are working in a custom manufacturing environment, it is always good to know how many projects are in the estimating stage. This tells you if your sales team is working and if they are talking to the right people, which can help you make adjustments.

5. **Who is generating those estimates?** If you have a team, sales metrics will tell you who is having success and who is not.

6. **What is the win/loss ratio for all estimates?** This is one of the biggest benefits. Knowing how many estimates you generate and what percentage you win is all you need to do to run the numbers and grow your business. From a profitability standpoint, if you are winning 100 percent of your estimates, you are probably priced too low. If you are winning none or very few, then your prices are too high. If you are winning 100 percent of your opportunities, congratulations; then you could, in theory, raise your prices. If you raised your prices by 25 percent and your win ratio only dropped 5 or 10 percent, it might be worth considering. If you have quotes that are repeat or similar to other quotes, you now have a pricing metric to use when pricing. See what data can do.

While you are trying to grow your business, you will also input your existing customers into the CRM system so you can start tracking progress in all your prospects and accounts. Again, if a CRM system is not in the budget, you can do a heck of a lot with a good old Excel spreadsheet.

If I had to recommend one tool that will allow you to manage your business, it would be a CRM system. The data alone and the decisions it helps you make are invaluable. Once you have a CRM system, it is easier to build a sales workflow using this technology, and the CRM helps to ensure your sales efforts are paying dividends.

Envisioning Your Workflow/Process of Selling

Internally, how an order is entered and processed in your company is critical. If a sales professional has to do it all, then that person will not be out selling. You probably can't afford that. In the printing business, entering and processing an order looks something like this:

1. **Sales:** Sales rep turns in credit application, signed quote, customer purchase order, and filled-out order-entry document.

2. **Customer Service/Operations:** Information is entered into the system to process an order.

3. **Customer Service/Operations or Sales:** Provide scheduling or turn-around time if a custom manufacturing product.

4. **Change Order:** If any changes are made in the process by customer that incur charges, sales should send a change order to the customer that documents the change so at final billing stage you capture this cost.

The internal workflow and process should allow for the sales person to bring in work, hand it off properly, and then go find new work while assured all the internal processes are working. Remember, if you, the owner, hire a salesperson, the more that salesperson is able to be out selling, the more money you will make.

Creating a Compensation Plan

If you are an owner and selling yourself, you may not feel the need to build a compensation plan yet. But if you are looking down the road, you may want to establish what you would be willing to pay a salesperson. It can be pure salary, a hybrid of salary and bonus, salary and commission, or 100 percent commission. You can also choose to outsource or work in a distribution model initially and work your way toward hiring your first salesperson. Hiring your first inside or outside salesperson is a big step, so best to ease into it when the time comes.

How do you make the transition from no salespeople to an outside salesperson that is paid on commission? Let me list a few ways to ease into it:

1. Start off by simply partnering with others outside your business to grow sales and build in an incentive. For example, if you are in the business of painting cars, try partnering or developing a relationship with a body shop that does not have in-house painting. Win/Win!

2. Work with a distributor. A distributor in your industry may already have a salesforce, and if you develop a partnership, its sales team could sell your products.

3. Start off with an inside salesperson who also handles some customer service work. Once the person builds enough business to be worthy of just focusing on sales, you can convert him or her to sales and create a full-time sales position.

If your compensation plan is not attractive, no one will want to work for you. If your compensation plan is too attractive, it may not be sustainable.

Remember, if your salespeople are bringing in *new* business, that means they are bringing in business you otherwise *would not have had*. Also, assuming your fixed costs remain fixed and your variable costs only increase in proportion to the workload, you are using your existing assets better. If you can keep your costs low as you grow your topline sales, you will soon come to a point where you will need to add machines, people, or both to support the new work. This is a good problem to have.

I have one last comment on figuring out a good compensation plan. You cannot overpay a good commissioned salesperson. Of course there are limits, but this is basically true. If you try to cut commissions, create a lot of arcane rules, or make it hard for a salesperson to calculate commissions, you will discourage sales-people from working for you.

Knowing How You Will Handle Customer Service

When you or your salesperson start to bring in new business, how will you handle customer service? Early on, you or the sales rep can do double duty and dote on the new customers. But at some point, you or your sales rep will be out selling and the customer will have questions, complaints, issues, a late delivery, status requests, etc. At some point, you have to make sure the customer experience from stem to stern or farm to fork is pleasant, as mentioned before. Happy customers tell five friends. Unhappy customers tell 500 friends. In the age of Facebook and other social media, those numbers may be quite conservative.

Technically, anyone in your business who has contact with your customers or prospective customers is in customer service. However, if you are going to set up a customer service department, here are few things I would recommend.

1. **Define what great customer service is:** I would first create a vision of what you want the customer experience to be and share that vision with your team. I would then recommend creating and documenting a customer service manual for all employees, even if only a few pages to start. It is important to make sure all new employees are quickly up to speed on what customer service means to you.

2. **Create a process:** How will you handle problems? How will you handle mistakes? How will you handle unhappy customers? There needs to be a process for your employees as well as an escalation path for your customers should they need to address a situation.

3. **Capturing data:** When customers are unhappy, how do they tell you? Phone, email, audio recording, survey? There are many ways to facilitate this communication, and depending on how your company is set up, it might be best to have multiple ways for customers to reach you.

4. **Hiring good people:** When hiring new employees, always incorporate customer service questions into your interview process. One of my favorites is, "Give me an example of a difficult customer service problem you have had and how you handled it." If you start off by hiring people you think are high quality people, you are simply making your job easier when it comes to training them. They will intuitively know how to treat your customers.

A wise man once told me that whenever you have an unhappy customer and a problem, you have an opportunity to make your relationship stronger. Similarly, I have heard that any company is a good company when things are going well, but the measure of a good company is how it reacts when a problem needs to be solved. Does it abandon the customer and avoid responsibility, or does it roll up its sleeves and quickly find a solution that keeps the customer happy? Creating a culture of top-notch customer service is the key to happy, long-term customers.

Creating a Sales-Driven Culture

Just like creating a culture of customer service, you must also create a culture that values sales and sales growth. Sales growth is good for the owner, good for the company, good for your customers, and good for the employees.

Too often when talking about a company culture, a belief exists that it refers to a large corporation, as if you need to have a certain number of employees for a culture to exist. I would argue a culture can exist in a corporation or a company of two people. I would also argue if you are a company of two people and you have plans to grow, you should establish the type of culture you want now while it is relatively easy to implement.

When it comes to sales culture, I find these days we have to use words like integrity, honesty, follow-up, determination, relentless, excellence, etc. The whole idea behind a sales-driven culture is never to be completely comfortable with your current sales. The 80/20 rule still holds true today: 80 percent of your revenue comes from 20 percent of your customers, and 20 percent of your customers will not be here next year. If any of your big fish customers are in the 20 percent, you need to be prepared to replace them.

In my own personal sales, when I land new accounts, especially accounts of size, I enjoy it for a month or so, and then I begin planning how I will replace these customers in case they leave next year. If you happen to work in a business based on repeat sales, this is great, but it is no guarantee your new customer will always be there.

Some of the biggest sales disasters I have seen resulted from salespeople who tore it up and grew their sales rapidly by sheer will or by landing one large account. They then got comfortable until life decided to throw them a curve ball. A customer jumped to the competition, cut back its ordering frequency, went out of business—the reasons are endless. Today, lazy salespeople who ride the wave and stop selling because they are making really good money are playing a risky game. The sales cycle can take days, weeks, months, or years. If you are not looking for new business each and every day when things are good, you, too, can be a victim of the "it will last forever" mentality.

Providing Effective Leadership

I saved leadership for last in this section. I did this on purpose because it is the most important topic, and I need it to be the last thing you read before we dive into the actual sales process.

Selling is about leading. Good salespeople are leaders internally and externally. Understanding this concept is critical.

If you are a business owner selling on your own, or if you are preparing to hire salespeople, it is your job and your job alone to create a leadership style that will not only set the tone but encourage others. Selling is not easy, and there is enough rejection to drive you crazy. Very talented salespeople get down and frustrated after they lose a big deal. Successful salespeople find a way to move on to the next opportunity quickly. Not all are able to move on as quickly, which is where you, the owner, must be the leader.

The old days of "my way or the highway" or "kick 'em in the ass if sales are down" can work, but it usually doesn't. Nearly all the salespeople I have known over the years are harder on themselves than most owners or sales managers, since their livelihood is at stake.

Some sales managers and owners feel that to be a good leader or manager, they must be tough and relentless, whipping the salespeople like race horses to get them to perform. This strategy is demoralizing and counter-productive.

As a small business owner, your job is to learn how to sell. Once you have the basics down, it is your job to decide whether you want to sell or run the business. If you choose to sell, you are going to become the sales manager for all new hires. If you elect to run the business and hire your first salesperson, you are still the sales manager until the time comes to hire a sales manager. Either way, you must understand how to sell before you can sell, you must understand how to sell before you can teach anyone else to sell, and you must create a sales environment where you can both inspire the sales organization you have just created and keep an eye on the overall customer experience.

You are the leader. In time, your salespeople will become the leaders in their account portfolios. Leading must occur for success to happen. Sales professionals lead their customers; sales professionals also lead internally to help their team support the customers. When this kind of leadership exists, everyone wins.

Never forget, being in sales requires leadership.

Summary

One of the most important things you can do early on is create a sales environment that is simple, intuitive, and scalable as your company grows.

Having a clear definition of sales and revenue helps everyone involved understand where the focus needs to be in a sales-driven company, and that is on sales. Clearly articulating how your customers will buy from you and what tools and technology need to be in place for you or your team to support your customers is critical. It is simply not enough to bring in new customers and figure it out as you go. For a company looking to grow, you must have an internal workflow, from order entry to customer service to project wrap-up, in place to allow you to support multiple clients at once seamlessly.

Creating a sales-driven culture is not easy, but neither is it rocket science. All you need is a vision and a basic, repeatable process in place—then you can add to the process as necessary.

Whether you are a company of one or a company with a small sales department, having a process in place is a sign of true leadership and vision for the future.

We have now walked through Section 1 of this book, "Pre-Sales Planning." Pre-sales planning may seem like overkill today, but when you begin to grow and add customers, you will be glad you are not creating a basic sales foundation on the fly.

In the remaining seven chapters, we will turn our attention to the actual sales process. Yes, we will start looking at and talking about the skills and techniques for actual selling. We will walk through each and every step in order to provide you with the flow of the process.

Exercise

1. Ask yourself, what do you want your sales culture to look like?

   _____

   _____

   _____

   _____

2. Sales and Revenue: Take a look at your business. What percentage is currently revenue that just comes in and what percentage is currently sale revenue you generate?

   _____

   _____

   _____

   _____

3. Do your customers know how to buy from you? What could you do to make it easier?

   _____

   _____

   _____

   _____

4. What tools are you missing that need to be in place?

_____

_____

_____

_____

5. What technology could you implement today to facilitate sales?

_____

_____

_____

_____

6. What part of your customer service solution could you start now?

_____

_____

_____

_____

7. List the attributes you as a leader feel are important as you add employees to your company?

_____

_____

_____

_____

SECTION 2
THE SALES PROCESS

Section 1 gave you a quick overview of the foundation you need to create a sales-driven organization. I hope you have already done this or are in the process of doing it as quickly as possible. As we've discussed, whether you are an owner planning on simply improving your sales skills or you are looking to hire a salesperson, it is critical that whoever is out there selling for your company has the support needed to achieve success. I have seen some pretty bad sales managers, and I have seen some owners try to "make" sales happen, only to get frustrated and not understand why sales are just not there or why the salespeople are not selling.

In my opinion, if you have talented salespeople or you yourself have a background in sales, but your sales are not where you want them to be, then one of two things are happening: 1) Either something is going on in the marketplace you are not aware of, or 2) The foundation or system in place to support the sales team is broken, demoralizing, or both. I have only spent three chapters on how to set-up the foundation for sales success, but I could have written an entire book on the subject (maybe someday I will). For now, however, I will move into the remaining seven chapters and walk you through the exciting, frustrating, and creative world of sales. I will touch on what works and what doesn't work from my perspective. Many of the skills and strategies I employ in the printing industry are relevant to all industries. Hopefully, after you have finished reading the remaining chapters, you will have a feel for and empathy for the sales profession. My hope is you will come to see that selling is really a process anyone can learn.

Becoming proficient in sales is like becoming an Eagle Scout. Not one Eagle Scout who ever achieved their status was born with all the required skills. A wide variety of skills need to be mastered to become an Eagle Scout. Each of the twenty-two merit badges are earned through practice and experience.

Like becoming an Eagle Scout, to become proficient at sales, there are skills you must learn, no one is really born with these skills. Each skill takes time and practice, but they are all very achievable. Gone are the days a salesperson must be "good looking" or a "smooth talker." Some of the best salespeople I have ever met are fairly quiet and introverted.

These days, customers are savvy. The internet gives them access to unprecedented amounts of data. If you are not a professional who understands the sales process; has empathy and understanding for your clients' businesses; understands business drivers, different business models, and how they make money; or how to create win-win outcomes, you will have a very difficult time.

Again, it's my belief that anyone can and everyone should sell.

Let's go....

Section 2 Highlights

1. Finding leads
2. Making contact
3. Getting the appointment
4. Performing a needs analysis
5. Presenting the proposal
6. Executing the sale

CHAPTER 4
FINDING CUSTOMERS

Leads, leads, leads. What's all the hub-bub about? How do you get them and where do they come from? Leads are said to be the lifeblood of all companies. Without leads, what would salespeople pursue? Finding leads is one of the more creative aspects of any plan.

What Is a Lead?

First, let's define leads in terms of B2B businesses. Sure, leads can be consumers looking to buy in a B2C environment, but in the B2B world, a lead is a contact or someone who is the buyer of a product or service from your company. This is the definition we will be using when discussing leads.

Bigger companies and corporations spend massive amounts of money to provide leads to their marketing and sales staff to follow up on. Marketing departments are constantly trying to figure out ways to get more leads to pass along to their sales teams.

For the small business owner, obtaining leads is how you start the process. And trust me; finding leads is where it all starts.

If I had to explain in one word my strategy for finding leads, it would have to be "creativity." That may sound odd, but in the following chapters, I will share some of my own techniques for finding leads. While some are pretty simple, some will flat out amaze you.

Before I start laying out the strategies for finding leads, I want to talk about scarcity. Yes, you heard me, good old scarcity. I am not going to go all "Econ 101" on you, but you need to understand early on that there is one scarce resource all business owners and good salespeople learn how to manage quickly. That scarce resource is *time*. It is said that the human brain cannot hold two completely separate thoughts at the exact same time. I know; cool, right? The same is true of a salesperson's ability to be physically in two places at the same time. If you are making a presentation at a customer's office, it is pretty hard to be somewhere else. I have always looked for ways to duplicate my efforts, be they through referrals, partnerships, or good old technology. So I figured that to be in two places at once, I had to figure out a way to clone myself.

I was looking for ways to generate leads in an automated fashion, or to have leads find me. After twenty-eight years, I only really want qualified leads or leads that have a pretty high percentage of relevancy.

Here is what I did: I went to the top five job-hunting sites. (Warning: If your boss sees you looking at job-hunting sites, be prepared to explain yourself.) I signed up for new automated job alerts. I typed in the following key words: print buyer, marketing manager, marketing coordinator, print procurement, publisher, marketing communications collateral, and last but not least, the name of my city, Seattle. (Remember, I work in the printing industry, so in your industry, the titles may differ.)

Now once a day, I get all job posts sent to me for those positions as if I am actually looking for a job, which I am not. By doing this, I am accomplishing two things: 1) I am verifying a company actually has people with the titles of the people I would normally talk to, which tells me it has printing needs, and 2) The company may or may not have someone in those positions currently, but someone is usually handling that role's duties while the company is looking to fill the position. Often, the people filling in are open to talking to new suppliers. So, while I am out talking to other customers all day, I have qualified leads coming in at the same time, so in effect, I have cloned myself! Currently, this method is providing about 3-5 good leads a week. That may not seem like a lot, but when you consider I am doing other things, like selling or sleeping when these leads come in, it is quite powerful.

Here are the benefits:

- I am now in two or even three places at once.
- I now know which companies in my area are hiring people who work with or buy printing.
- I now know they either don't have someone in that role, or they are adding a person to that department. Either way, this new person is usually far more willing to talk to a new guy than the existing buyers or marketing folks who have programs up and running with other printers.

Of course, the leads all come in, and I must sift through to find the ones worth my time, but that only takes minutes. As you can see, creativity in finding new ways to generate leads is the name of the game.

Qualifying Leads

All leads are not created equal, and all leads do not end up generating revenue. When I was a new salesperson, one of the biggest frustrations I found was working on a lead for hours, days, or weeks, only to find it was not really a good lead after all. It is imperative that you find a way to qualify the lead you want to pursue as a solid lead.

What is a solid lead?

- **A lead that fits your company.** If your average job value is $50,000 and the company you are calling on is a $70,000 company, there's a good chance this lead is too small for you. Conversely, if you are a 1-2 person company generating $300,000 in gross sales, you may find many companies are simply too large for you to support well. Also, most companies have different requirements, i.e., quality, pricing, turn-around time, etc. Identifying companies whose needs and requirements line up with your company's expertise will yield far better results for you and your potential new customer.

- **A lead that buys what you sell.** Many times when we see a company, we are forced to make educated guesses about what it does and what it buys. This is fine, but you must quickly find a way to figure out if it truly buys what you sell.

- **A lead that has a need you can fill.** Later on, we'll talk more about how to conduct a needs analysis. For now, just remember most customers buy when they have a need, so if you can uncover one or more needs during a meeting, it really helps to qualify a lead. For example, you identify a customer who buys what you sell, you have seen his work, and you know you can improve his quality. During the meeting, if he tells you the quality is "good enough for us," then that need may not exist, or at best, may not be compelling enough, so you must restart the process and probe to find other needs to qualify this lead.

Qualifying leads is important so you don't waste valuable time. Time is one luxury small businesses typically don't have. If you are going to run the business and sell, you had better be very efficient at both. To be the most efficient, I suggest looking for leads that are in plain sight.

Leads in Your Backyard Are Usually Already Qualified

Before we go into detail about how to uncover leads and where to find them, I have to start with three techniques that seem simple, yet many fail to do. Before you start randomly looking in the phone book, here is what you should do:

- **Industry Verticals:** If you are a B2B business, and you are already fortunate enough to have a variety of existing customers, then start there. If you have success with automotive, construction, or insurance clients, then start your search by identifying all companies in those spaces, and mine specific industries you know you have already had success in.

- **Your Competition's Customers:** If you have competitors, go to their websites. You would be surprised how often in some industries companies list whom they do work for, especially if it is for other large, brand name companies. While this is meant to show credibility to site viewers, it is an opportunity for you to see who is buying products and services from your competition instead of you.

- **Referrals:** While we will talk more about referrals, always ask your good customers for referrals. Offer them a Starbucks gift card for a referral. This show of appreciation can be very powerful.

Note: The key here is to get traction quickly. If you are calling on companies you already know buy what you sell, and that are currently using your competition, then you know you are not wasting your time. To me, this is the easiest way to get qualified leads or leads you know are worth spending time on. Some like to call this "low hanging fruit." While I understand the need to try to make this process simple or easy, I find the term "low hanging fruit" is not a good description. Nothing is easy or simple, and every opportunity requires effort. Yes, starting with companies that you know are qualified is faster, but only because you are not in the qualification stage very long, and you can skip right to the "getting-in" stage and know you are not wasting your time.

Now let's look at some other ways you can find leads.

Social Media

Many social media sites claim to generate leads for small business: Facebook, LinkedIn, Spokeo, Twitter, YouTube, Google+, Pinterest, Ryze, Talkbiznow, Affluence, Quora, etc. In my experience, LinkedIn and Spokeo are the two best for locating the correct contacts within a target customer. Most of the others are simply places for a small business owner to publish content to try to attract customers—more of a B2C approach.

LinkedIn is far and away the most beneficial lead generation tool I use. In the old days before the internet, no real way existed to figure out whom to reach out to within a particular organization. You had to call and ask for someone in purchasing or procurement or for buyers. With LinkedIn, you can greatly narrow down the potential contacts and, in many cases, find the correct one with 100 percent certainty.

So how do you use LinkedIn? First, you sign up for the least expensive membership you can, currently at around $65.00 a month. Trust me, it is well worth it. It may be possible to start with a free membership, but the bare minimum is limiting. Keep in mind that LinkedIn is best for penetrating larger companies. But today, many people at small companies have LinkedIn profiles as well.

The following is a short list of how I use LinkedIn to find contacts and leads.

1. If I have identified a company I would like to research, I go to LinkedIn and type in the company name. It usually gives you someone from that company, and from there you can see who that person is connected with. You can usually produce a handful of contacts. Then try to narrow your list based on the job title and description.

2. If you already have customers, look them up. Not because you need them, but to investigate whom they are connected to. Often, buyers, procurement folks, and marketing folks hang out with others in their industry.

3. If you have a contact name, try entering the person's name, city, and business name in Google. This search will usually either pull up the exact person or someone else in the company. You can look again at the person's contacts to see if any look like the one you want.

4. You can try to reach out to people directly on LinkedIn, but I have not done this. I only reach out to people I know or have made contact with.

5. Once you have identified the person you think might be the correct contact, check just under his or her photo. Sometimes people list their contact info. Usually, it says to contact the person through the company website, but sometimes you get lucky.

6. Another trick is to see where the contact went to college. I went to Western Washington University. Whenever I see a fellow graduate, I try to start off with that association or use the phrase, "from one Western alum to another."

7. You can also gather information by seeing where someone worked in the past. You may know someone within one of those companies who could help you.

LinkedIn can be a wealth of information. Sometimes I can sit down and in 20-30 minutes develop a pretty large stack of good leads. In fact, leads can stack up so fast you can almost forget to stop compiling them and start actually calling some.

Depending on your business, you may find other ways to use LinkedIn to create leads and contacts that will help you grow your business.

Referrals

Referrals can be a great way to leverage the good work you have done for your customers. Some customers will refer you without any prompting; others will require you to ask. One note of caution here: I always advise to do a good job first before you ask for a referral. I know this sounds obvious, but I have seen the reverse happen. It is awkward for a customer to give a referral if you have not done any work yet. The customer doesn't want to be rude, but has not seen you in action yet, so is not a happy client, yet.

Assuming you have happy clients, there are two primary ways to approach referrals:

1. **Just ask:** When I have done a good job supporting my customer, I tend to quip, "Hey, I buy lunch for referrals." It is more of a passing comment, but I am planting the seed nonetheless.

2. **Set up a program:** You can make your referral program part of your everyday communication. You can send follow-up emails reminding your customers, like real estate agents do. "I make my living by referrals." You can also set up a drip campaign: Every quarter you send out an email talking about past projects and asking customers if they know anyone in their circles who might need the same services.

A word of caution: Never use the name of your customer when talking to a prospect without getting the customer's permission. I had the misfortune once of simply saying, "I was talking to Bill over at XYZ company about what we do for him, so I thought I might give you a call to see if I could introduce myself." As you can see, I did not say Bill sent me, but if a customer "assumes" Bill sent you, it can be uncomfortable. Always get permission before you name drop.

Hoovers

The website www.hoovers.com is a great tool that allows you to get a lot of information. However, in my opinion, it is more geared toward finding out information regarding corporate clients. It is still possible to get information about smaller companies, but just not quite as easy. Because there is an ongoing fee every month, it is important to make sure you and/or your sales team are using this tool a lot to justify the expense.

ReferenceUSA Database

While Hoovers will require an outlay of cash, I prefer to use the ReferenceUSA database. Not only is it free, but it is an excellent research and lead generation tool. While you can purchase it, there is an old school way to get it for free. Go to your local public library—I really meant old school. Most libraries will grant you access if you have a library card. I know what you are thinking, "I don't have time to hang out at the library." Not to worry; you don't have to. With my library card, I simply go to the library website, click on databases, enter in my library card number, and voilà, I can access the database from anywhere.

This database is quite handy and uses the SIC codes to sort data. You can do some research in the database to identify which SIC codes you wish to look up and either save them to your computer or print them out. Note: One of the unusual restrictions is that you can only download or print up to 250 records at one time. Try for 251 records and it will kick you out for twenty-four hours. But, again, don't worry; you can download 250 records as many times as you want; just don't go over the 250 batch maximum. You may want to consult with your library to ensure the 250 limit is the same.

One other key: After you select and print/download 250 records, make sure you go back and deselect those records before moving on to the next 250. Once, when I accidentally deselected all but one record from my previous search, the system thought I was downloading 251 records, so I was kicked out.

Why is this tool helpful? It is free, it sorts by industry SIC codes, it allows you to build lists, it allows you to search geographically, and it provides contact names and other key information that will help you drill down and create good lead lists.

Trade Shows

Trade shows are a mixed bag. They are usually pretty expensive to enter, and they are rarely in your town, so travel is often required. You must also possess a booth, which can get quite expensive. If you are going to use travel shows as a lead generation tool, here are a few things you might want to consider:

1. Make sure your staff at the booth understands the mission. Make sure everyone is on board and understands the goal of the trade show is to get live hot leads to pursue. This can be done by having a session with your team to discuss what information you want to collect and how you are going to go about it.

2. Collecting information from those who visit your booth is critical. The old business card in the fish bowl is a bit outdated, but if you can make it interactive, that always helps. Drawings, sign-up sheets, and information request sheets can all be paper-based, or a tablet can be set up for those who prefer digital. The key is to know who your prospects are and what they want to learn from you.

3. Questions are one of the best ways to help determine why someone is visiting your booth. Each person working the booth should ask the right questions to narrow down the information you are seeking.

4. If there is a handout bag that trade show attendees receive as they enter the venue, get something in that bag with your name and number on it. If you can make whatever it is something really cool or useful, that is even better.

5. You can also attend trade shows as part of the audience. Sure, having a booth at the trade show is one way to gain exposure and get leads, but if you simply attend, it is usually free or low cost and there is always something to be learned.

With the advent of the internet, trade show attendance has declined, but there are some really good companies putting on some well-attended events that can still be useful. If you do it right and keep good notes, at the end of the year you can look back and see how many clients came from these events and then calculate your return on investment. You may find it is well worth the effort, or you may find it is not the best process for you and your business.

Book of Lists

Every city in the United States has a publisher that publishes a *Book of Lists*. This is simply the top 50 or 100 biggest employers, biggest public companies, etc. in the area. These books are considered old school, but they do provide a pretty detailed list of your local area and who is doing what. They often provide contact names you can run through LinkedIn to generate leads. These books are not very expensive and usually well worth the small fees. Many of them are also available with a membership through the publisher.

Direct Mail

While direct mail has its place, it is typically more of a shotgun approach. But if you are good at taking notes and creating data (lists), your direct mail efforts will be much more targeted. If you are not good at making your own lists, you will need to provide specific criteria to a list broker who then provides you with a list of prospects in a specified geographical region. These lists can be really good or really bad, but either way, they charge per name. On top of the list purchase, you have to develop a compelling direct mail piece, have it printed, and measure the results. Direct mail is an effective strategy for B2C as well as B2B. The key is to make sure your piece is compelling, targeted, and has a call to action.

In the digital age, the ability to personalize and create 1:1 marketing pieces for each recipient has made this less of a shotgun approach, but the numbers don't lie. Traditional direct mail has about a 1 to 1.5 percent response-rate. If you do a good job personalizing and making each piece relevant, I have heard the response rates can be as high as 20 percent. The problem is that companies that get great response rates are not always willing to share what the rate is or how they achieved it. It can be considered sort of a trade secret, and rightly so.

I once saw an extremely successful direct mail piece. A large trucking company that sold semi-trucks kept good data on the people who bought its trucks. The company knew exactly what truck each customer bought, what model, and even what color.

This company also was keenly aware that truck drivers only make money when they are on the road driving. They only drive when their trucks are in good running order, and you guessed it, oil changes are the primary form of maintenance. So, after each truck purchase, a four-panel postcard went out in the mail to the truck owner. It had a picture of the customer's exact truck on the front panel, and when the customer opened the mailer, on the inside was a map to the nearest oil-change location to the customer's address. It even showed how to park when you pulled in to save the jockeying around. The card was also a coupon for one free oil change. As you can imagine, the revenue generated in future oil changes and other maintenance was massive. All it took was some careful planning and understanding the customer's needs and this program kept customers coming back.

Not all direct mail is this effective, but it is still another good channel to consider.

Networking

Networking is one area I have to admit I am not the most proficient. Have I done it? Yes. But do I do it a lot? No. This is not because it doesn't work; it's more about my personality and style. As I mentioned early on, I am a bit of a shy person in these situations, and shy does not cut it. If you love to mingle and chat, and are one of those who can find a way to meet everyone in the room by the end of the night, go for it. Some very good contacts can be made if you have the talent and skill. Networking isn't my forte. Find what works for you and capitalize on it.

Several types of networking exist:

In-Person Networking:
- Industry trade shows
- Breakfast networking
- Meet-ups and happy hours
- Conferences
- Conventions
- Host your own event—an event such as a lunch and learn

Online Networking:
- Meetup.com
- Alignable
- LinkedIn
- Twitter

Some people view the concept of networking as painful. However, if you take a friend or spouse and have a plan to mingle, meet new people, and make connections, it can be a very good way to be more visible locally and leverage your selling efforts. Nothing is better than going to a networking event and then the following week have someone call you who says, "One of my friends attended the networking function and told me we should connect." (Note: Always find out who referred the person to you and then thank that person. Referrals are a big deal and should be treated as a big deal.

Networking has many benefits, but the primary benefits are making local and long-term business connections and becoming engaged in the local business community.

Some Dos and Don'ts:

1. Make sure to take business cards.
2. Make sure you follow up if you tell someone you will.
3. Look for opportunities to help connect others. These connections will come back to you.
4. Be polite. Handing out business cards to everyone in the dinner line is sort of rude.
5. Don't just tell everyone about you. Be curious and ask others about what they do.

More Non-Traditional Techniques

To illustrate the creativity aspect of looking for leads and contacts, I am going to share a couple of my unique approaches. Of course, my background is in the printing industry, but these ideas will hopefully inspire you to come up with some creative ideas of your own.

1. **Issue.com Approach:** Issue.com is an online digital magazine website. It lists hundreds to thousands of magazines on its website that you can view free of charge. Keeping in mind that magazine printing is one of the product types I work with, I simply go to the site, type in Seattle publications, and voilà, up pops a screen full of local publications. Once there, I simply go to the editor's box, where it lists the name and address of the publication and provides a website address. If it is indeed local, I go to the company website and look up the media kit to find out the

size, page count, frequency, and run quantity. Once I have this, I know if it is a lead worth pursuing. Most times it is. This may seem like a simple idea, but no one I know is doing it. By taking the time to do this, I am increasing the odds in my favor dramatically when I do reach out. The more you know about your prospects, the better the odds you will be relevant when you contact them. Of course, I do this same thing for Portland, Sacramento, San Francisco, Los Angeles, and Boise, Idaho.

2. **"In the News" Approach:** When I am looking for a name or contact info for a specific marketing person, I simply go to Google and type in "<name> in the news" or "director of marketing for <company name> in the news." In the first case, when I have a name, I am looking for a press release. Marketing folks get interviewed a lot for new product releases or noteworthy changes at a company. Marketing people like to connect with their market so, quite often, at the end of the article, they list their name, phone number, and email address. Bingo! I have what I need to reach out. If I do not have a name, then by typing the company name followed by "in the news," I usually get the name if there are any press releases. These are just a few tricks I use to sleuth out people who are key decision makers and sometimes difficult to reach.

3. **FSC Approach:** In my industry, FSC stands for Forest Stewardship Council. People who buy printing and want to show they are environmentally responsible put the FSC logo on their printed pieces. It is required when you use the FSC process that there be a chain of custody. On the logo is a number through the FSC representing the printer who printed it. When I am trying to uncover who my competition is, I simply go to FSC.org and do a reverse lookup to see which company printed a certain piece. If it is someone local, that helps me. If it is someone in Asia or the Midwest, that too helps me. If the competitor is someone I know I can compete with or beat, and often do, that changes how I introduce myself and my approach when reaching out to

a customer. For example, if I know I am always a lower cost than a certain competitor, I might lead with the cost savings I know I can provide.

4. **Chambers of Commerce Approach:** I was once asked to see what I could do to develop a relationship with Microsoft, located in Redmond, Washington. I had no contacts, so as you might expect, I was running into a stone wall at every turn. Those folks are pretty good at being accessible only when they want to be. I decided to take a different approach. I looked up the Chamber of Commerce in Redmond and in every outlying town and city around it. My reasoning was that people like to be involved in their local communities. When they get involved at a chamber, they almost always list the company they are with and their contact information. If they decide to join a committee, even better. I came up with twenty-five leads this way and took those twenty-five leads to LinkedIn, coming up with nearly a hundred before I got what I needed. Long story short, that year, I did nearly $500,000 in sales with Microsoft. It may seem like a lot of work, but when the payoff is large, the time spent is money in the bank.

Summary

As you can see, there are traditional methods for lead generation and nontraditional creative ways to pursue the prospects you identify as good leads. I personally find it a huge challenge to find creative ways to identify and gather data regarding an account and/or a contact. I consider it a huge compliment when I am asked how I find new leads. My customers ask, "How did you find me?" My boss asks me, "How did you find this account?" I usually respond, "I could tell you, but I would then have to kill you." Finding leads that your competitors don't find is a rush.

Regardless of how you find leads, you must find a way to build a lead list if you are going to have new business to pursue. To me, this is the best part of the job, and I consider finding leads an art form. It is a very creative process, and the more creative you are, the more success you will have.

Finding contacts and companies to pursue is one thing, but actually reaching out to them is an entirely new skill you will have to learn in order to grow your business. "Getting In" is an art form— one I have perfected over the years.

As you will see in the coming chapter, "Getting In" is where sales professionals really earn their money. Every opportunity and proposal has to start with an introduction. In this day and age where people are busy and move around, this is not easy. I will again show you some of my tricks and strategies for getting in, getting in at the right level and with the right person to begin the sales cycle.

Exercise

1. Where is the best place to find leads?

   _____

   _____

   _____

   _____

2. How can you use social media to generate leads?

   _____

   _____

   _____

   _____

3. What is your best source of referrals?

   _____

   _____

   _____

   _____

4. What technology platforms might help you generate leads?

   _____

   _____

   _____

   _____

5. Which event could you attend to find a way to begin networking?

_____

_____

_____

_____

CHAPTER 5

MAKING CONTACT

At some point, you will actually have to make contact with potential customers. Some call this cold calling, outbound sales calls, networking, telemarketing, etc. Regardless of what you call it, this is where the sales process really starts. Finding leads is more research-focused; making contact and taking action with the lead is the human part of the sales process, and it is critical that you understand this quickly.

Honestly, I do not like the term "cold call." To me, it sounds like telemarketing, a cold introduction, a shot in the dark, or a shotgun approach. Cold is negative. I prefer the terms "outreach," "making contact," or to sum them up, "demand generation." While you can call this process anything you like, I think it is important to use terms in line with a positive mental attitude and professional approach. I am far more excited, or if you wish, far less fearful, of demand generation than I am of the dreaded "cold call." I think how you frame this process really makes it easier or harder for you to take action. Here lies the fear many speak of when they think of sales. If demand generation removes the fear and helps you take action, then demand generation it is.

Why do I use the term demand generation? If you were to Google the top ten or twenty reasons business owners give for failure in small business, lack of demand for their product is always in the top ten. But what does this mean? Simply put, when money comes in, it is viewed as "demand." When no money is coming in, it is "lack of demand" from a mathematical or economic point of view.

Let's face it; effective salespeople bring money into a business. Similarly, creating demand has the exact same effect. If someone off the street walks into your business and places an order for $1,000, or if through a sales process you bring a new customer into your business who spends $1,000, can't both be seen as demand from a business viewpoint? Yes, $1,000 is $1,000, regardless of how the demand was created. Does it really matter how the order came in? Yes, it really, really does if you want to learn how to sell on purpose.

My first sales job was with Nordstrom in Bellingham, Washington, selling ladies shoes. A friend of mine suggested I work there because it was great pay for college students. With no sales experience, I wondered if I could do it. After I met with the sales manager, I was hired.

Let me be clear; Nordstrom is a wonderful company. What I am about to tell you is more about what I learned from passive retail sales than about Nordstrom. But the sales process at Nordstrom is what set me on my path.

About four to five salespeople worked a shift. We had a makeshift line in the back where we all waited our turn to assist a customer. When the first customer came in, the first salesperson in line approached her and went to work. We then took turns. Once it got busy, it was a free-for-all. Those who could greet, finalize a sale, and ring it up quickly, got to move on to the next customer and make more money. When the store was having a sale, this process was sort of like a shark-feeding frenzy with everyone busy working.

The problem is that this passive sales process is fine during a sale with lots of foot traffic, but what happens when it slows down, or it is a regular day without a sale? You spend a large part of your day waiting your turn to approach someone and maybe secure a sale.

It was during one of these slow periods, when I was doing busy work while waiting for my opportunity to go sell, that I realized I would rather bring customers in than simply wait for them to maybe come in. I realized I could sell, and I realized I liked working with people, but I was simply too impatient to passively hope someone walked into the store so I could start working. This is probably similar to how most shoe stores work. I learned that passive retail sales were not for me. Any experience can be helpful when you learn from it and apply what you learn in your career, which is precisely what I did and still do today.

So, how do you actually make contact? How do you start the demand-generation process? Keep in mind this is a creative process. The more creative you are, the more successful you will be. If you simply approach a prospective customer like every other salesperson, you will find your odds of success lower than if you look for creative new ways to meet prospective customers.

When all is said and done, only a few methods of outreach will really get you in contact with a prospective new customer—the phone, letter writing, a trade show, and email. What really counts is the technique you employ. Here is a list of some techniques and tactics I have found to be effective with these methods.

The Phone/Voicemail

The phone is probably the fastest and quickest way to get a conversation going with a customer. It is also the fastest way to reach many prospective customers in a single day. However, it is one of the scariest ways for those learning the sales process to reach out. Whatever you do, be prepared. You should always have a plan for a live conversation and a backup plan or script ready in the event you get voicemail.

With a few tricks, phone calls can be effective and even fun. The higher up the food chain you are calling, the less likely you will be to get the person on the phone on the first call. Often you will be sent to his or her voicemail. Don't fret; this is a victory as long as you have a compelling voicemail message already scripted.

I once heard the story of a salesman who found a way to overcome his fear of making "cold calls." He simply kept track of his outbound calls for a month. He calculated how many calls he made and how much money he made. He then ran a test for a quarter. The results were that for every phone call he made, he earned $22. Yes, every call. If he called someone and that person became a customer, it was worth $22. If he called and the line was a disconnected number, he still earned $22. If he called and someone hung up on him or yelled at him, it earned him $22. That's right. If he stuck to his call schedule, every call would yield $22 at the end of the year. Granted, he was in the insurance business, where 99 percent of sales come from dialing phone numbers all day, but this was an effective and creative way to take the fear out of rejection, provide motivation, and create a positive experience.

Let me tell you the story of about a lead I pursued that eventually became one of my best customers.

In 2004, I placed a call to the senior buyer at a large comic book publisher to introduce myself and see how I could get involved with printing comics. The buyer, while a little skeptical, asked me what type of presses I had. I gave her a quick overview of our presses. After I finished, she said, "Call me back when you have the right type of equipment," then abruptly hung up.

Fast forward to 2014. I had moved on to a company that had the perfect press. Not only could this press hit the price point, but it could fulfill the challenging quality requirements as well. I got on the phone and called the buyer. After a few days of trying, she finally answered.

"Yes, who is this?" she asked.

"Greg, Greg Andersen calling you back," I replied.

"Do I know you?" she blasted.

"Yes," I said. "In fact, five years ago I called you and you asked me what type of presses I had. After I told you, you said, rather bluntly, 'Call me back when you have the presses I need.'"

She replied, "I did? Okay."

"So, I am calling you back because I now have the presses you need," I said. I then proceeded to tell her about our unique presses.

There was a long pause; then as abruptly as ever, she said, "What is your email? I have a few projects I will send your way to give you an opportunity." We exchanged emails and the call was over.

Within an hour, I received requests for proposals for three different titles. Excitedly, I wrote up the estimates she requested. This was no easy feat since I did not have a lot of experience yet at my new company. When I presented these proposals, I was awarded all three. The first job was $82,672 for 162,900 comic books. While I was pleased with my efforts, my company was floored at this rather large order. Now, you must understand that the average job at my company was around $5,000, so this was a substantial order—and by the new guy, no less.

My new boss, the owner of the company, wanted to know how I had done this. First, he asked, "Was this an existing client you brought with you?"

"No," I replied. "I never worked with this customer before." No need to explain about our 2004 conversation; it would only reduce the mystery of what I had accomplished and how I had done it.

He then asked, "How did you reach out, make contact, and get moving so quickly?"

"I can tell you," I said, "but then I would have to kill you." In all honesty, I simply told him I had identified the company's VITO (Very Important Top Officer), called the front desk, and asked for her. Once I had her on the line, I told her I had a press that delivered what I like to call "extreme value." When asked, I explained that extreme value simply meant *"the best quality at the best price"* and that she would benefit greatly if we could explore what this press could do for her.

My boss, a little bit dumbfounded, said, "You just called her? And two weeks later, you had your first job and an $83,000 first job at that?"

"Yes," I casually replied. "That is exactly what I did."

Fast forward again to the end of 2014—the tail-end of my first full year at this company. After producing many more comic book titles with flawless execution, I ended up earning my company $235,000 the first year, and in my second year, $350,000 from this one new customer. It was all because I kept meticulous notes, made a phone call, and painted a picture of what my press could do for the buyer—add value.

Sometimes a simple call and being bold and straightforward are all that is required to uncover a great opportunity.

Here's what I learned from this experience:
- Keep good records.
- Make the call and be fearless.
- Do your research and make sure you are not wasting your or your prospect's time.
- Paint a picture of the value you can provide.

When reaching out to a new customer, you need to have a plan that covers the following four criteria:

- **Call objective:** You always need to have an objective—secure a face-to-face appointment, make a sale on the phone, get permission to send some information or literature, or get permission to call back at a better time. This may seem obvious, but trust me, I have heard of many calls going south because there was no objective. The primary objective of every call is to get an appointment. In your business, this may be different, but for me, face-to-face is where the big deals really happen. But first you must get your customer's attention; then you must start a conversation, and your conversation must be relevant. It is amazing how fast a prospective customer can hang up if you start off poorly, have called the wrong person at a company, have nothing relevant to say, or have not done your homework.

- **Call location:** You need to be in a quiet place without distraction. You need to focus, be prepared to take notes, and, if all goes well, reach your objective. Barking dogs or coworkers talking in the background make it hard to focus.

- **Call position:** I prefer standing over sitting because it gives me energy. Either way, you should be prepared to take notes and have any materials you need on the call in front of you.

- **When to call:** This takes some trial and error. Obviously between 9:00 and 11:30 a.m., and from 1:30 to 4:30 p.m., are the golden hours during the day, but there are a few exceptions I like to use.

  1. **Early/late calls:** When I am calling an owner or senior executive, I often call between 7:00 and 8:00 a.m. and 5:00 and 6:00 p.m. Most hard-charging owners or senior level contacts are hard workers and arrive early and stay late.

  2. **Lunchtime calls:** At some companies, getting past the gatekeeper (usually a receptionist) is virtually impossible. How-

ever, at lunch time, they too must eat. A backup receptionist is usually not as challenging as the regular one. This situation can be effective in two ways:

a) If you do not know who the decision maker is, you can simply ask, "Who handles the_____?" If the receptionist tells you, ask to speak with that person. If the receptionist won't put you through, simply jot down the name and call back later.

b) The same applies if you know the name; ask to speak to that person. If the receptionist says he or she is not in or won't put you through, call back later.

In both cases, if you are fortunate enough to get sent to your prospect's voicemail, be prepared to leave a compelling message.

What to Say on a Call

The fastest way to end a call is to start off poorly. Here is my approach.

1. **Identify yourself:** "Hi, Greg Andersen calling from XYZ."

2. **Be polite:** "Is this a good time to call?" If not, find out when would be a good time. If yes, let the person know why you are calling.

   a) "I saw your company in the news and…."
   b) "I was passing by your office and always wanted to stop in and say hi…."
   c) "I use your product and was wondering if we might discuss…."
   d) "I have a unique process that helps my customers save money and time…."
   e) "I understand you are looking to…."

f) "I see from your LinkedIn profile you went to Western Washington University, so I was hoping as one alum to another I could introduce myself…."

g) "I work with many customers just like you and wanted to share how we help them save money, time…."

h) "I see you won an award for…."

i) "I was talking with [name drop here] and he/she thought we might be a good fit…."

j) "I have a unique solution that no one else has…."

k) "As a business owner, I understand…."

l) "The economy is bad, but my solution…."

Note: Keep in mind you must have some reason to call. You must get the prospect's attention.

3. **Be brief:** Once you have them talking, *let them talk.* I can't emphasize this enough. Do not interrupt; do not assume you know where they are going; stop talking, and aggressively listen. You must also realize that not many people these days have much time for a long unannounced call. At some point, you must move toward your objective. Here are ways to do so:

a) "Do you have time to grab coffee and discuss…?"

b) "How can I show you my process for…?"

c) "Would you like me to send you some…?"

d) "Is there a better time for a longer discussion…?"

e) "What would it take to get a few minutes of your time…?"

f) "I would be happy to meet you wherever is convenient for you…."

g) "I have a demo that I think you will like…."

4. **Don't un-sell yourself:** If you have determined that you will not get any further, find a polite way to stop the call. If you have reached your objective, also stop. Close the call politely and set up the next action. You can easily "undo" a positive call by staying on a call too long.

a) "Great, how about next Monday at…."
b) "I would be happy to send you some information…."
c) "Oh, Joe Blow handles that? I will reach out to Joe…."
d) "Yes, I can call back in June just before your current contract expires to discuss further…."
e) "I understand, and I appreciate you taking my call…."
f) "Thanks. If you ever find yourself in need, please do not hesitate to call…."
g) "I am glad to hear you are being taken care of. Should things change, I can be reached at…."

5. **Voicemails:** In-person calls allow you to ask questions and have a discussion. Voicemails, on the other hand, are a one-sided message. If you do leave a voicemail, you need to be prepared with a script memorized or on paper that allows you to leave a compelling message that will prompt a return call.

a) "Sorry I missed you. I was speaking to Jane Doe and she felt we should meet…."
b) "If you are looking to save money, I have a solution you may not have heard before…."
c) "Your competitors are using my products/services, and I thought you might want to see why…."
d) "I understand your business/industry and have a unique process for improving…."
e) "If the economy is causing you pain, I have a solution…."
f) "I have many customers just like you who are benefitting from my…."
g) "I have a case study I think you might want to see…."

Note: Always leave a way to contact you in a voicemail. It does no good to leave a voicemail and not leave your name, number, and company name.

Contact by Letter

While a letter may seem like an old-school strategy, it is a very important part of any outreach strategy. Remember, in every outreach program you must be relevant, and to be relevant, you must reach out to your customers in the way they want to be reached—letters, emails, trade shows, FedEx, networking, association meetings, direct mail. Advertising is very similar in that consumers cannot all be reached the exact same way. When advertising, you probably won't just advertise in one form, right? Advertising takes many forms—online, print, newspaper, Yellow Pages, blogs, white papers, association websites, etc. Yes, I actually listed newspapers. Why? Well, depending on whom your potential clients are, their age group, and how they consume content, you very well may need some or all of these channels to reach them. Yes, even newspapers, if that fits your business.

If you are going to write a letter, not just any letter will do. Two of my all-time favorite sales books are Anthony Parinello's *Selling to VITO* and *Think and Sell Like a CEO*. *Selling to VITO* includes a chapter on how to write a VITO letter. I highly recommend this type of letter to everyone who intends to use letters as part of a contact strategy.

What is a VITO letter? First of all, as stated earlier, VITO stands for Very Important Top Officer. As in any contact strategy, your goal should be to identify and reach out to the proper person as high up the food chain as possible. If you can, call the owner, CEO, or general manager. But keep in mind that every business is different. Sometimes the VITO is the Director of Marketing or Director of Purchasing. What you are looking for is the person who has the decision-making authority, and that person is different in every company.

Let's talk briefly about what a VITO letter looks like. In Figure 1, you will see one of my VITO letters. Over the years, I have made a few tweaks, but I recommend you follow the VITO letter carefully until you have a full understanding of how it works.

"For five years in a row you have made me look great. You have a 100 percent on-time delivery record, and always deliver excellent print quality! With you, and the team at Consolidated Press, I know the EG Conference Program will be flawless, arrive properly packaged, and in perfect condition."

— Christopher Newell, Event Designer,
Entertainment Gathering

Jane Goldsworthy
Senior Marketing Specialist, Print Production

Jane,

Would you like to know how we hit 100 percent on-time delivery for our clients? Well, quality, pricing, on-time delivery, results…that is what we do.

If any of the following are on your to-do list, I may be able to help:

- Obtain sheet-fed quality with heat-set web pricing
- Reduce overall printing costs while increasing quality
- Print on unique substrates up to 40 points thick
- Reduce turn-around time and get materials in hand faster

We are running two unique presses that virtually no one on the entire West Coast has, which allows me to provide what I like to call "extreme value."

Our value proposition is "excellent quality and the best price" and we do it every day. When you are balancing tight budgets in a competitive retail marketplace, you must have both.

I will call you soon to see if we can talk further about how we help our customers save money and improve quality.

Sincerely,

Greg W. Andersen
Business Development Manager
206-769-3974

Figure 1: Vito Letter

This is the letter I sent to a very large pet hospital lead back in 2014. After sending this letter, I followed up off and on for more than eighteen months without success. Then, out of the blue, in June of 2016, I received a call from Jane. She said, "Greg, this is Jane at the pet hospital." Okay, I was caught a little off guard. At first, since I am actually a customer of this pet hospital, I thought I had forgotten about an appointment to take Dexter, our wiener dog, in for a checkup. But she went on to say, "I did get your letter and voicemails, but I was not ready to talk then. Now I am ready, and I would like to start a conversation about how we may be able to work together." Finally, my brain snapped back, and I realized this was a response to the letter I had sent nearly two years earlier.

Fast forward to today. I provided two proposals for two projects and won both of them to the tune of $235,006 in one month. To put this in perspective, my average sales goal with all forty of my accounts is around $125,000 a month. The average job at my company is around $5,000–$6,000. The average of my first two jobs was a staggering $117,503. What you cannot see is that when you add these sales to my other sales, I was at about $409,000 for the month. I only needed $125,000 a month to meet my goals. Since I get paid quarterly, another way to look at this is that $409,000 per month equals $136,333 per month, for three months. In other words, this month covered my entire quarter. While I am always excited by good sales, the owner of my company was ecstatic. Sure it was $235,006 of sales revenue, but the real reason he was ecstatic was threefold.

1. This was brand-new business. Business my company's owner did not have the month before.
2. A nice account at our company is $100,000–$200,000. This was just two jobs.
3. This job prints four times a year!

If is not clear by now, this single letter generated a huge amount of revenue for very little effort.

This letter has worked time and time again. Along with the pet hospital, this letter helped me succeed at companies like Hewlett-Packard, Microsoft, Ancestry.com, Wanful.com, and Costco, just to name a few.

So, why does this letter work? Here are a few of the basic reasons:

1. **Header:** I provided a testimonial of a similar happy customer to gain credibility.
2. **Introduction:** The introduction is designed to get attention.
3. **Bullet Points:** My research led me to believe these items would get her attention.
4. **Something Unique:** I briefly mentioned my unique presses that no one else has.
5. **Summary:** I let her know I would be reaching out to set up an appointment.

One of the real strengths of this letter is that it is brief and to the point. While she may not be the CEO, I did find out she is the primary decision maker, so she was the VITO. The concept of the VITO letter is that CEOs and VITOs do not have a lot of time to read long, two-page letters. You need to get to the point quickly.

As I have mentioned, there are many ways to reach out to a customer. So, when should you use the VITO letter? I use the VITO letter usually to reach out to large, high-value potential clients. Yes, I really only use it for large strategic accounts with C-level people. This letter requires some research and a testimonial from a similar client, but if you have these two things, the process can yield great results. In my first-ever attempt, I sent out ten VITO letters and received five callbacks, three appointments, and two new accounts. One of them, the HP opportunity, turned into a three-million-dollar contract account!

Contact by Email

The VITO letter is the slowest outreach approach and the phone is the fastest, but email is the second fastest. Many folks avoid calls or have their receptionist screen them, but everyone sorts and deletes his or her own email. Like phone calls, you have the briefest of moments to get someone's attention, but you have direct access, assuming you can get the person's email address. How do you do this? What do you say? The following is a list of things I personally do to find email addresses, and once I find them, what I say to get a response.

First, you have to find email addresses. These can be easy or just downright impossible. Following are the methods I use to try to get ahold of email addresses.

- **Company Website:** If your prospective customer is a senior executive, you can often find this information on the company website.

- **Associations:** If you have a prospect you met at an association meeting, members are often listed with contact information, especially if they hold board positions in the association.

- **Google "(Company Name) in the News":** This one I invented. I am often looking for marketing folks, and when you simply google "Jane Doe in the news" or "(company name) in the news" you will see press releases often given by marketing folks, owners talking about new product releases, and new happenings. These press releases often list name and contact information.

- **Contact Websites:** Many sites (e.g., Hoovers, Lead411, Spokeo), if you pay, will provide you with names, numbers, and email addresses.

- **Trade Shows/Events:** If the prospect is at a trade show or event, get his or her card. A name badge with a title on it will tell you if you have the right person.

What to Say in Your Initial Email

Now that you have the person's email address, since you have never talked to him or her before, what do you say? How long should your email be? Should you send attachments? These are all good questions.

The reason I bring this up now is that I have taken the VITO letter and developed my own VITO email that gets fantastic results.

Remember, VITO stands for Very Important Top Officer. The concept is, to sell effectively, you must sell at the highest level and to the correct person. You must speak that person's language, you must understand something about his or her business to be relevant, and you must be short, sweet, to the point, and grab the VITO's attention quickly.

As you can imagine, if this works in a written letter, then with some modification, it can work in an email format as well.

Figure 2 is just one example of a VITO email. A little context here will help. I sent this email to the owner of a company that publishes educational planning booklets for students and teachers. Below is the very first email I sent the customer on May 1, 2014.

To: John Smith
From: Greg Smith
Subject: Publishing Customer

"For five years in a row you have made me look great. You have a 100 percent on-time delivery record, and always deliver excellent print quality! With you, and the team at Consolidated Press, I know the EG Conference Program will be flawless, arrive properly packaged, and in perfect condition."

— Christopher Newell, Event Designer, Entertainment Gathering

Attn: John Smith

Would you like to know how we save our customers money and deliver world-class printed projects on time with no surprises?

If any of the following are on your to-do list, I may be able to help:

- Reduce printing and freight costs
- Reduce turn-around times
- Use the correct press for the project (digital, roll-fed, sheet fed press, or heat-set web press)
- Work with a print/mailing partner that understands value and how to create it for the education industry

We are running two unique presses that virtually no one on the entire West Coast has, and they allow me to provide what I like to call "extreme value." Our value proposition is "excellent quality and the best price," and we do it every day. I will call to see if I can possibly show you a solution you might not have seen before.

Sincerely,

Figure 2: VITO Email

Result: John responded to this email on June 3, 2014, with curiosity. On December 14, he arranged a tour. On January 9, his team came to my office, took a tour, and discussed their business. On November 18, 2015, I received word that we would be getting our first titles in to print in April 2016. This may not seem quick, but the value of this account is $200,000-plus. Again, in my business, where the average order is $5,000–$6,000, this was a huge sale with a contract to boot. It proves my VITO email really works.

As you can see in Figure 2, I start off with a testimonial from a happy customer, followed by an explanation of how I could do the same for the prospective customer. Then I list items I know are important to publishers and are often pain points, and I close with my company's expertise and a promise to call, as well as my contact information.

Let's look at the individual parts of this email and why they're successful:

- VITO = Owner/decision maker
- Happy customer testimonial = credibility
- Bullet point issues = relevance
- Unique presses = unique solution
- Claim to fame = value

Contact by Fax

Honestly, contact by fax is not something I recommend. At one time, many strategies were used to reach out to prospective customers through fax, but I have always found faxes to be ineffective and impersonal, plus there's no real way to know who is picking the fax up off the machine. And in 2018, not a lot of faxes are being sent. While I felt I should mention fax as a form of contact, I would stay away from reaching out to prospective customers by fax.

Contact at Events/Trade Shows and Networking

In-person networking is a great way to meet prospective customers. Personally, I find that business never gets "done" at trade shows, but contact does. I would be more apt to call trade shows lead-generation opportunities. Lead generation is very important; no targets mean nothing to shoot at.

Trade shows require more tact if you are going to be effective and not come off as a hack or amateur. To illustrate this point, I want to share my Microsoft story. I once sat on a fishing boat with the chief decision maker I needed to talk to for nearly eight hours before I made my move. My boss was scheduled to go on a sturgeon fishing trip with a bunch of industry executives, but a conflict arose, so he asked me to take his place. This event was located at the mouth of the Columbia River, just off the coast of the Washington-Oregon border. Not knowing anyone who would be there, I arrived early to get to know people beforehand. The first person I met was Steve from Microsoft. I introduced myself as a print salesperson, and he introduced himself as the vendor manager in charge of hiring, firing, and monitoring all print vendors for Microsoft. Talk about being at the right place at the right time. At that very moment, it would have been so easy to go into sales mode, but something told me that would be the wrong approach. Remember, never sell too early. So Steve and I, and a group of about twelve in total, fished, drank beer, and talked all day long. Because I had met Steve first, we developed a comfort level and talked on and off most of the day.

The dilemma was how to make something out of this situation. I felt if I did not at least walk away with something, I would have failed as a salesperson. As we inched closer to the end of the day, I started trying to come up with a nice way to say anything that would position me to talk further about business. I purposely did not bring it up all day since no one was really talking business, just fishing and relaxing.

As we were motoring into port, I was running out of time. Once we hit the docks and everyone dispersed, I would have missed my opportunity. Here is what I did: As we were approaching the dock, I simply said, "Steve, you know, I have to tell you that my boss would absolutely kill me if he knew I spent all day on a boat with you and did not ask for the opportunity to talk further about supporting Microsoft?"

"Well," Steve replied, "what exactly do you do?"

Prepared with my two-minute irresistible sales pitch, I simply talked about our value proposition and how, depending on the direction Microsoft was heading, we might be able to support its efforts. Steve responded by giving me his business card and saying, "Absolutely. Call me next week to set up a meeting." I was ecstatic! It had been painful and scary, but I had done it simply by asking to have a follow-up conversation.

Fast forwarding to the results of that conversation, I had my meeting and began the odyssey of becoming a Microsoft Vendor. This was not easy and took lots of time and effort for me and my team. The first opportunity we were involved in was an online web-to-print portal and fulfillment opportunity valued in the millions. Unfortunately, we did not win; a Canadian firm won. But by the end of the year, I did manage to sell nearly $500,000 in direct mail printing. Was taking the risk on the fishing boat worth it? Heck yes!

Because these types of situations develop with little or no warning, I feel it is critical to be prepared for face-to-face, spontaneous meetings. Had Steve asked me what I did and I'd frozen or not been very articulate, the results may have been very different. If you are attending events, here are a few dos and don'ts you may find helpful:

1. As a salesperson or business owner, do be prepared to explain what you do in under two minutes. Contacts will ask you, and you need to be able to provide a quick overview of your busi-

ness in a big picture way.

2. Don't forget to reciprocate. If someone asks you what you do, you must ask that person the same question. It makes him or her feel you are interested, and it starts your research into whether the person is a valid lead for you.

3. Do bring business cards, but be judicial about whom you hand them out to and how you do so. Do not be the person who runs around handing out business cards to everyone in the dinner line. Remember, unless everyone can become a customer, you must try to meet, understand, and quickly qualify whether a person is someone you need to talk to further.

4. Don't be shy. Just like the Microsoft fishing trip story, it is not easy for some people to strike up conversations with strangers at an event. Remember, most events require badges, and most people at these events are there for networking, so they expect others to introduce themselves. So, roll up your sleeves, strap on your courage, and go shake a hand.

5. Resist the temptation simply to hang out with familiar people you know. Your goal is to meet new people, and this event is good practice.

All in all, while trade shows and events are good places to network, to me, the time commitment alone tends to mean they are not the most cost-effective or reliable way to find and get in touch with new clients, unless the attendees happen to be a specific group of people who are all a good match for your product and services. For the right event with the right people attending, it is an excellent place to develop leads and practice networking.

Social Media as Contact Strategy

As mentioned back in Chapter 2, using social media is a good way to reach out to your customers. While it may not be in person, you can start a conversation and have a dialogue that can ultimately lead to driving sales. As we noted earlier, Facebook, LinkedIn, Twitter, YouTube, Pinterest, Tumbler, ETSY, and many others are simple ways to begin a conversation and drive people to your website or physical location.

In fact, I would argue that, if done right, you can actually reverse the sales process. Picture this: Instead of reaching out to a customer and trying to sell your product after exposure to your social media content, what if the customer called you and asked you to sell your product to them? What if the customer, rather than you or your sales team, initiated the sales process? Here is where I think the true power of social media lies. I call this "customer-driven sales," or when your customers demand you sell them something. It is sort of an odd way to look at sales when your customer is both customer and salesperson. However, if you do it right and implement a rewards program, one customer could also bring others to you.

While social media will create a conversation and can generate leads, until the time comes when social media drives your customers to you, you will still need to have an outbound sales process in place. Part of that process requires you to reach out and personally talk to your customers. The question is: How do you do this? How do you actually "get in" to start the conversation?

Summary

Making contact is critical to starting off the process. As you have seen, there are several ways to make contact. You simply need to figure out what works best for you and then do it. As you get more experience, you may even be able to tell what works best for your customers and if it is good for you; if it is, then you have the home run. Make sure when you do reach out that you have a plan and you know what you want to say. Remember, phone calls generate fast results and letters can generate slower results; it all depends on the customer you are reaching out to and your preferred style—both work. And last but not least, leveraging social media sites in your outreach efforts can pay off if you have a strategy and a plan.

Once you get in contact and have a conversation, you will need to figure out how to convert "contact" to "appointment" or whatever your next step will be. The following chapter will start exploring ways to "get in" so you will have an opportunity to start the sales process.

Exercise

1. In your business, what are the best ways to reach out to your leads?

   _____

   _____

   _____

   _____

2. Take some time to write out a script for a person-to-person call and a script that would work if you reached voicemail on your call.

   _____

   _____

   _____

   _____

3. Create a few letter templates in advance that can be repurposed quickly. (Feel free to use the VITO letter.)

   _____

   _____

   _____

   _____

4. What social media platforms could you use to reach new prospective customers?

_____

_____

_____

_____

CHAPTER 6

GETTING IN

Finding the Correct Person

Can you imagine a shooting range without any targets? Can you imagine a football game without any end zones? Before you can develop your "getting in" strategy, you must first figure out the target, or who are you are trying to get in to see. Getting in just for the sake of getting in is a surefire way to get tied up for months and months talking to the wrong people and stalling or ruining your sales efforts altogether.

I once spent nearly a year calling on a company, getting moved from person to person, until one day I accidentally met someone who was the specific person I needed to talk to. From that point on, it did not take long to secure my first order.

What's in a name? If you can get just one name within an organization, you have substantially improved your odds of finding the correct person. Many ways exist to ensure you identify and focus on the proper person when reaching out to a prospective customer. What follows is a helpful list of ideas, but feel free to add to this list for your own industry or particular process.

- **Social Media:** As mentioned in Chapter 4, social media tools these days are very helpful when it comes to quickly identifying a small group of people within a company or department to start narrowing down your search. LinkedIn, Alignable, and Spokeo are just a few. My go-to resource is LinkedIn. On LinkedIn, it is pretty easy to identify people in marketing, operations, procurement, IT, and many other departments. Once you identify them, you will see whom they are linked to. Sometimes the person you find can lead to many others in the same department. Often, after finding the person you think *is* the best contact, you realize others connected to him or her are actually better targets.

  - I once found the VP of Marketing and figured: Why not start there? Upon checking who the VP was linked with, I found the senior marketing coordinator had a bio that went into full details about how she managed all the printing and distribution for the entire company. Since my position was focused on print-related sales, this quickly shifted my focus off the first person and onto the coordinator. That said, sometimes the VP is the best place to start. I am a big fan of starting as high up in the organization as possible. Sometimes, based on circumstances, going directly to the decision-maker may or may not be the best path. It's for you to decide what will work and give it a go.

- **Direct call:** Depending on the nature and size of the company I am trying to work with, I have often simply picked up the phone, called the front desk, and asked who handles the print purchasing at the company. You would be surprised how often the person will either tell you or put you on hold to find out. Once you have a name, you have a target.

- **Lead Generation Sites:** As previously mentioned, Hoovers, ReferenceUSA, and Lead411 are just three of many lead-generation sites that allow you to do research prior to making contact. Some of the sites, like Hoovers, do have a subscription fee, so you have to figure out if your needs justify the cost. The ability to generate a list of targets can shorten the sales cycle, which is always good.

- **Google:** One of my other methods is to use Google. Let's say I am looking for the director of marketing for the Port of Tacoma. I simply type into Google "Director of marketing for the Port of Tacoma." When I did this, "Tara Jones, Communication Director" popped up right away.

When you go to Tara Jones's LinkedIn page, you will see she is connected to five other employees at the Port of Tacoma. If you click on each of those contacts, they too have four or five other employees at the Port of Tacoma they are linked to. Your ability to leverage one name into thirty-five additional names means you have an excellent pool of people to reach out to, and you simply have to figure out who is the best one to start with.

Note: Here is another little trick. Remember, there were five other contacts within the Port of Tacoma on Tara's LinkedIn page? Well, there were a total of eight contacts on her page, but three were not within the Port of Tacoma. Most marketing people are friends with other marketing people at other companies, so I now had three other possible leads at other companies to pursue. While this process is great for finding people within a company, it is also a great tool for finding people who are marketing directors as well!

The Art of "Getting In"

After you have figured out the best person to reach out to and have gotten his or her attention, either on the phone, in an email, or at a trade show, how do you convert this new contact to an appointment? Finding the right person seems like a lot of work, but the real work comes after you have made contact because you need to know what to say.

I once heard a story that goes like this: After repeated attempts to reach a prospective customer by phone, a salesperson finally resorts to having a cactus delivered to the prospect with a note attached. The note reads, "I have tried getting you on the phone, I have tried emailing, I have tried writing letters, and I even talked to your secretary who said you were traveling and not always in your office, so I thought since you are rarely in your office, you might like a plant that does not require daily watering."

It's a funny story, but it illustrates what I feel is the single biggest reason people are successful at getting appointments and, ultimately, new accounts. If I had to pick just one word, I would pick "creativity." Whenever I am asked to name the most important quality in sales, specifically new business sales, I always come back to creativity.

Based on this chapter's title, you have probably guessed that one of the biggest challenges in sales is getting in or penetrating an account, and then, subsequently, what to say once you are in. Getting in is an art form and a very creative process. Yes, there are tried-and-true methods we all know about, and they do work. But keep in mind, if you know about them, everyone else is using them too. If you want to be different, you must think of yourself as an artist. If you had received that cactus and note, you would probably remember it the rest of your life. It would probably be the only cactus you ever received. See my point?

Yes, it is difficult to find prospective customers. Yes, it is difficult to reach out and make contact. Once you do, the even harder challenge is how to get in. By getting in, I mean setting up an appointment and then actually having the meeting. Face-to-face is where the sales process really begins. Sure, there are ways and times to close deals on the phone, via email, or via letter. However, to truly develop a relationship and do the research/leg work to develop new business, you must get face-to-face. Your odds of success go up exponentially every time you are able to get face-to-face and begin or continue a dialogue with your prospective customer.

The following are a few of my own personal stories about how I got in that might help you understand the creativity approach.

Hewlett-Packard

I once came across a website that looked like a good lead and a good fit for what my company did. However, when I looked closer at the site, it had the little HP logo indicating it was a division of the monstrous company, Hewlett-Packard. It was a Friday, so I decided not to waste my time on such a long shot. By Monday morning, I had changed my mind. It just so happened that my company owned the largest install base of HP Indigo presses in the printing industry, so I figured, "Why not leverage that?" I went to the website, looked up the VITO, who happened to be the general manager, and sent him an email. Not an ordinary email, but a very creative, well-crafted email. I called it my "Wouldn't it be cool if" email. I figured he probably got calls all day long, but since he was a tech guy, an email might get read. I would only get one shot, so it had to be good. It took me about an hour to write that darn email, but it turned out to be the most important letter of my life. First, I did a little research to ensure that my assumptions or educated guesses were relevant, since I had never met with or worked with anyone from HP. Remember, you really only get one chance to make a good first impression. What I did was paint a picture of what a partnership with me and my company would look like and how they would benefit from such a relationship. Below are the highlights of my vision.

Basically, I wrote a brief letter saying, "Wouldn't it be cool if...?" and then painted a picture of what could be:

> What if HP could use my "HP" network of 256 presses based in Asia, the United States, and Europe to support its client base more efficiently? What if I could steer your customers' work to under-utilized presses, so not only would you have the fastest turn-around time but realize the best pricing due to my company's desire to fill low spots in production? Wouldn't it be cool if instead of shipping finished product from the United States around the world, you could email pdf files to one of our plants in that country and produce and ship locally, saving money and time?

I received a response that very same day. It simply said, "I like the way you think. Call me in thirty days and I will be ready to have a discussion about your vision."

I called in thirty days. We had a contract in two months and began generating revenue in three months. The sales revenue in the first year was $300,000. By the time I left that company in 2014, the revenues on that account had climbed to over two million dollars. Now, that may not seem like much, but in the digital printing world, that is a pretty good-sized account, and it is still growing. It is also worth noting that this is a program type account. In other words, if set up properly, a program will keep running and generating revenue even when you are doing other things.

Children's Magazine

In 2008, I called on a publisher in Santa Cruz, California. My first call ended quickly; she told me she had another year left on a contract and to call back next year. So, in 2009, I called a few months earlier than I had the year before, but she said she had just signed another contract. Fast forward to 2014. I was at a new company. I called her even earlier in the year. This time she said she had a contract and that she had used the same printer for fifteen years. At this point, I got a little bold and said if I did not think I could make a substantial impact, I would not have called. I asked her just to let me take part in the request-for-quote process that year. After all, what did she have to lose? She agreed. We had a contract signed within a month of the proposal. It turned out I could save her $2,000 an issue on a six-issue magazine publication.

Microsoft

Back in Chapter 5, I talked about how I made contact with Microsoft through a fishing trip. That story is a great example when it comes to getting in. Many times, we get the person on the phone, or grab coffee with him or her, but getting in means figuring out a way to build rapport and become a trusted partner. In the Microsoft story, I made contact, but my real dilemma was finding a way to convert this opportunity to an appointment, and ultimately, a request for proposal. As you saw during that fishing trip, I used my boss as a lever to try to make me feel a little bit less intrusive. If I said my boss would have had my head for not asking for an appointment, it was not really me asking, but my boss, and that strategy worked. As you will see throughout this book, being creative in your approach is critical. No two situations are ever exactly alike.

Salon Services NW

Back in September 2014, I was getting a haircut when I looked down at the stack of magazines next to me. The one on top was *View Points*. I turned it over and saw that the indicia (mailing info) said Renton, Washington. Bingo! It was a local company, which meant my unique press was even more unique. I rushed home and looked up the magazine on LinkedIn, but that was a dead end. I googled "Viewpoints Magazine pdf" and found them. (Most publishers create online or pdf versions of their publications these days.) I opened the pdf and noticed the FSC logo. I took the FSC code, went to FSC.org to do a reverse lookup, and found out who the magazine's printer was. It was a printer I could easily beat. I called the company but got a recording, of course. So I called my hair stylist, who gave me the name of the regional salesperson who handled her account. I called her, and she gave me a name to call at the corporate office. I called back and put her name into the company phone directory, but that was a bust, since no names were in the company directory.

I went to Google to see if she was there—no good. I called the headquarters number again and pressed one for customer care. I said I was looking for Suzanne Smith and was transferred. She was not in. I did this a few times at different times of the day, and finally, I reached Suzanne. She was not the right person, but she she told me that Shelly Jones was the correct person.

I ran through this process again and, of course, got Shelly's voicemail. Fast forward. After three to five calls, I waited a bit and called on March 27, 2015, nearly seven months after I started. I had to go again to customer care and ask for Shelly, but this time I actually got her on the phone. She was hesitant at first, but the call ended with her requesting samples, a proposal, and telling me what I must do just to be considered. First, my price could not just be a nickel less. It had to be worthwhile to upset a solid partner she was already using. Second, at a minimum, I had to be able to meet the same quality. Third, I must be able to produce the magazine in 7-10 days.

As you can see, this process is very creative. It almost requires a detective-like process to uncover the right person. Just like water running downhill seeks the path of least resistance, you must look for every angle to find a way in, and then be prepared to deliver a quick, compelling reason to talk further. Nothing is more frustrating than going through this difficult and sometimes long process only to lose the customers' attention when they ask, "What do you want?" and "Why should I work with you?" While not all cold calls are successful and it can be easy to get frustrated and even a little negative, be prepared when you do have success.

While the above stories are all good examples of getting in, I think the Hewlett-Packard story illustrates the importance of being relevant when trying to make a connection. I personally believe that understanding how to get in is the single biggest factor in success or failure. You must create a starting point on which to build. The first step is to reach out; you need action to start the sales process. If a customer says yes or no, both are actions. Better to get a quick no and move on than tie yourself up for months, only to get a no in the end. To my way of thinking, a yes is best, but a quick no is not bad either. As I once heard, "Never take no from someone who can't say yes." In other words, if you are not talking to the correct person, you are wasting your time. In the next section, we will discuss whom you need to be talking to so you can get in and see the right person.

Getting an Appointment

How do you set up an appointment and convince someone to take an appointment with you? It's a three-step process.

- **Preparing for the call:** Do your research and homework. If you are calling a company, you must have figured out it is a good prospect. Why? Can you save them money? Can you improve their quality? Can you produce faster than the competition? You must understand as much as you can about who the prospect is, what they need, and why you are uniquely positioned to provide a solution for their needs. It takes research and some educated guessing to get someone to agree to sit down and meet with you.

- **Scripting:**

    - **Talk Track:** It is often a good idea to create scripts for calls in advance. Note: I never recommend reading a script; memorize and practice it so often that it comes out naturally. When you do this, you never do it the exact same way twice, but you have the general flow down, so you are prepared.

    - **Have two different scripts:** Have a script for if you get the person on the phone and one for if you get voicemail. While you can use one for both, I have a slightly different one I use when I get someone live on the phone.

    - **Be relevant:** If you are relevant, you stand a better chance of having a productive conversation. When you're talking to a marketer in the banking industry, look up terminology unique to the banking industry. If you speak the person's language, you can develop what is called an equal business stature, and you are more likely to keep his or her attention.

- **Making the Call:**

    - **Be comfortable:** Sitting or standing, do whatever works best for you.

    - **Make sure you are not disturbed:** You need to focus.

    - **Put notes on your desk:** Plan for questions in advance. For example, if you are calling a bank, one question you might get is, "What other banks do you work with?" It is a good idea to have a list of other banks somewhere on your desk. Also, people in the same industry often know each other. If they are in banking, they may also ask if you know some-one at another bank. Notes are important. This is a bad time for your memory to fail you.

- **Be high energy, but not too high:** Don't be a cold fish on the phone, or monotone. Simply be conversational and nat-ural. It can take practice. You will make mistakes, but after practicing for a while, you will find it gets much easier and feels much more natural. One trick I like to use when prac-ticing is to record myself on my cell phone and then play it back to see how I really sound. You would be surprised how much different you sound when you play it back.

- **Block out time:** If you try to make calls sporadically throughout the day, that can work. I find if you dedicate a few hours, or even half a day, to just reaching out, you get in a groove and get better faster.

- **Ask for the appointment:** At some point, you will have to ask for the appointment. Make it easy for people to say yes. Often, I say, "I will be in the area on Wednesday and would be happy to stop by, meet at your office, or meet at a coffee shop nearby." Promise to keep it short. If the meeting goes well and the prospect wants to keep talking, they will let you know. When you do get the actual appointment, if they originally told you that they only have thirty minutes or an hour, make sure to check in at the thirty-minute or one-hour mark. Simply say, "You told me thirty minutes, and I just want to be respectful of your time." If the conversation is going well, the prospect usually does not kick you out at this point.

- **Persistence:**

  - **Rejection:** If every call resulted in an appointment, sales would not be as challenging. Be prepared for a flat out no. Sometimes you have a discussion and sometimes prospects simply hang up or flat out tell you they don't have time to talk.

- **Follow up:** This is where the sales process takes effort. If the person says no, ask if you can follow up at a later date. If they say not now, then ask to follow up at a later date. If you do ask and the response is "okay," you *must* follow up and state, "You told me to follow up, so I am following up" when you contact them. This reminder is a good way to jog someone's memory since she may get a lot of calls.

- **Creatively staying in touch:** If you get a no, but you are convinced the prospect is a good lead for you, you have to look for ways to reach out again in the future. Send samples or an email newsletter with interesting articles. If the person truly is a good lead, you need to be professionally persistent and find a way in.

- **Enough Nos Eventually Lead to a Yes:** It is simple math. Remember the story of the insurance agent who calculated how many calls he made and how much money he made— every call he made, regardless of a yes or a no, equaled $22 in his pocket.

Note: Generally speaking, about 45 percent of salespeople give up after one call to prospective customers. In sales, it can take five to seven calls or conversations to land an order. Persistence is critical.

Summary

Remember, the goal is to get the prospective client's attention. If you are prepared, comfortable, relevant, and have a compelling reason for meeting the person, the chances of setting up a face-to-face meeting are greater. As you have seen in some of the preceding examples, being creative and looking for any way to connect with the right person is critical. Always be prepared to alter your approach based on circumstances. Finding a way to convert that contact to a meeting or a tour of your company is also a surefire way to kick off the relationship.

In the next chapter, we will explore what to do in your first meeting. Getting a meeting is great, but sales is a process, and each step in the process leads to the next step. You should always have a plan for the next step.

Exercise

1. What are the best ways to reach out to your potential customers?

    _____

    _____

    _____

    _____

2. In what ways can you make it easy for a client to meet with you?

    _____

    _____

    _____

    _____

3. What social media tools will best fit your outreach efforts?

    _____

    _____

    _____

    _____

4. What time of day would best be devoted to making calls to set up appointments?

    _____

    _____

    _____

    _____

5. When you get a prospective client on the phone, what will you
    say are the reasons for exploring a relationship with your com-
    pany? Make a list.

    _____

    _____

    _____

    _____

CHAPTER 7
GETTING AN OPPORTUNITY (THE APPOINTMENT)

The Appointment

You have done everything right, and now you find yourself at your first appointment with a new customer. Now what? What do you say? What do you do? How do you prepare? What is the goal of the meeting? Like any new situation, this can feel stressful, but remember, this is fun stuff—you are in the process of growing your business. You need to get in the right frame of mind.

I want to talk briefly about the sixth sense. Yes, I know there are really five—sight, sound, taste, touch, and smell. I personally believe to be good at sales, you need to develop what I like to call the sixth sense—*empathy*. Simply defined, empathy is the ability to understand and share another's feelings. Affective empathy is also called emotional empathy, and with practice, you can learn to respond with the appropriate emotion that will demonstrate empathy to other people's situations. While many argue that empathy is something you are either born with or not, I am a firm believer that anyone can learn how to show empathy, and it is extremely helpful in sales.

How do you incorporate empathy into your selling? While not easy, it is possible. Here is what you can do to increase your understanding and use of empathy which will help you immensely during the sales process.

1. **Listen Aggressively:** In order to truly understand, you must listen aggressively. You must focus. Whoever you are talking to should be able to *see* you listening. You cannot ask good questions if you are not listening.

2. **Walking in Another's Shoes:** How do you feel someone's pain? Ask yourself how you would feel if this were your problem. Think of a time when you had a similar pain or problem and ask yourself: How did I feel?

3. **Be Curious:** Good questions show you are listening. You must find a way to get into the discussion to fully understand everything you can about the person and his or her problem. In order to demonstrate empathy, you must ask questions that show you, too, understand the problem and the pain it causes.

4. **Acknowledge Pain:** When you acknowledge that you see the pain someone is feeling, you bond with that person. Never skip past real pain or problems. Ask whomever you are talking to how this pain affects her and her business. Pause to show you are focused on them.

5. **Apologize to Bond:** By apologize, I mean when someone tells you a loved one has died, don't you say, "I am so sorry to hear that"? Saying, "I am so sorry for your troubles," "I am sorry you are having a bad experience," etc., does not mean you are the cause so it's

not really an apology. But using "I'm sorry" does help you appear closer to being the one who can provide a solution.

6. **Share a Vision:** There is always light at the end of the tunnel. Once you are fully engaged and you have heard, discussed, and shared the pain/problem, you always need to wrap up on a positive note. "Let's see how we can fix this," or "I have an idea that just might solve your problem," or "I will do my best to solve this problem for/ with you" are just a few ideas.

Developing some level of empathy is crucial to developing the relationships you need with your potential customers to ensure, first, that they will become customers, and second, that you will have a long-lasting relationship.

While this book is based on my personal approach to creating and growing sales, I think this is a good time to share with you the various types of selling methodologies that currently exist. No one style works for everyone, so I think understanding what processes and methodologies are out there is helpful. I think it is also my responsibility to expose you to a variety of processes so you can best determine what will work for you. When you are actually at the appointment, you will need to have a process or a plan for how to move through the sales cycle.

Sales Methodologies

First, what is a sales methodology and how does it differ from the sales process?

•   The sales process is a stem-to-stern outline, or an end-to-end process, for identifying, engaging, communicating, and ultimately on-boarding a new client.

•   A sales methodology can be a stem-to-stern approach or it can simply be one aspect of the sales process, like finding leads or asking good questions. A sales methodology tends to be an opinion on *how* to sell and what actions to take at specific times with your prospect.

If you take the time to look up the methodologies and books I will mention below, you will find that in some cases, my personal approach probably takes a little from each. If I read a book or study a method that I think will enhance my sales efforts, I test it first, and if it adds value, I adopt it. If not, I don't. Sometimes I simply select parts of a sales methodology that make sense to me and ignore the rest.

As with anything else, people have been selling many different ways for years. Be aware—there are a lot of gimmicks and a lot of people out simply to sell a book. While I feel there is always a nugget of gold in every book or methodology, you still need to be on the lookout for bad advice. Personally, I always learn something valuable in every book I read or methodology I explore. You just have to select carefully what seems valid and ignore the gimmicks. There is no silver bullet or magic ingredient in sales, no matter what people tell you. While some methods are good, some are not nearly as valid. The key to remember is if a method gets results for you, then use it—if not, don't. Remember, not everyone sells the same way, or even the same way to every single customer.

A Quick Overview of a Few Different Sales Systems

- **SPIN Selling:** Nick Rackam introduced SPIN selling. It's focused on the four questions a salesperson should ask and the order in which they should be asked: Situational, Problem, Implication, and Need/Payoff.

- **N.E.A.T Selling™:** Developed by Sales Hacker and the Harris Consulting Group, N.E.A.T. Selling is a qualification process: Needs, Economic impact, Access to authority, and Timeline.

- **BANT Selling:** Originally introduced by IBM, it stands for Budget, Authority, Need, and Timeline.

- **ANUB Selling:** Developed by inside sales as a lead-qualification methodology, it stands for Authority, Need, Urgency, and Money.

- **Conceptual Selling:** Known as the Miller Heiman approach, conceptual selling says salespeople should not lead with a pitch for a product, but first understand what the buyer's concept of their product is. Again, this process has a list of questions: Confirmation Questions, New Information Questions, Attitude Questions, Commitment Questions and Issue Questions. This process focuses on listening and breaks down the process into three distinct sections: Getting Information, Giving Information, and Getting Commitment.

- **SNAP Selling:** This methodology by Jill Konrath seeks to keep the buyer and seller on the same level. The acronym stands for keep it Simple, be iNvaluable, always Align, raise Priorities. This methodology assumes there is not one single decision in the sales process and SNAP selling can keep the process on track.

- **The Sandler System:** This system is sort of a flip on the traditional sales process. Instead of the salesperson convincing the buyer to buy, the buyer will end up asking the seller to sell. This is accomplished by quickly uncovering all needs and associated pain upfront. If the seller cannot really provide a solution, then the seller is done. If there is a good solution, then they proceed.

- **MEDDIC:** Created by Dick Dunkle and Jack Napoli, this acronym stands for Metrics, Economic buyer, Decision criteria, Decision process, Identify pain, and Champion. This process is more geared toward enterprise or complex solutions sales.

- **FAIR Sales Method:** This method is based on specific types of questions and the order in which to ask them. The acronym stands for Fact, Anxiety, Impact, Result/Reward.

- **Challenger Selling:** Created by Brent Adamson and Matthew Dixon, this approach assumes the salesperson is one of five personas: hard worker, reactive problem solver, lone wolf, relationship builder, and challenger.

- **QBS selling:** Developed by Thomas Freese, QBS stands for Question Based Selling. This process is based on discovery and qualification by asking not just questions, but good questions, at the right time, and asking them of someone who has the answers. Listening is an important aspect of this philosophy.

As you can probably imagine, I could list more than I have, but I think you get the idea. While some of the acronyms get a little lengthy, they are excellent when trying to come up with a quick title for a book or a simple way to remember a sales process. If you take the time to research these methodologies, they will teach you a lot. You will also notice they have a lot of common themes, such as the importance of questions. Nearly every sales process correctly focuses on how to ask the right questions, the right way, at the right time, of the right person.

What you will also notice is some of these models are a little out-of-date, and some seem almost manipulative in some cases, so I really suggest you take what fits and leave the rest. I also caution you to be careful in selecting just one and running with it, unless it really satisfies every need you have.

While I will walk you through what to do during a first appointment, I would like to share a story about what not to do in a first meeting. The following story happened to me, but hopefully, will not happen to you.

Full Color Samples, or Never Show Up and Throw Up

As a young salesperson, many lessons must be learned the hard way. That's not to say the easy way will not accomplish the same result, but the hard way tends to create a lasting impression. But, before I can tell you the story, I need to explain what is meant by "show up" and "throw up." Many salespeople show up to a meeting and, due to their inexperience, simply start talking and don't stop even long enough to ask questions or to let the customer talk. As we will learn later in this book, asking good questions and allowing your customer to talk is the key to understanding your customer's needs. But if you simply barf out a presentation that is all about who you are and who your company is, and you ignore or forget to involve your customer in the discussion, you are guilty of the dreaded show up and throw up syndrome.

The following real-life story illustrates this concept.

I had been working on a very large account, which was known to spend millions of dollars on printing. I had worked hard for several months, and finally, success. This new customer had agreed to an introductory meeting to talk further about his business.

Like any rookie, I gathered my literature. I assembled the highest quality full color samples I could find to showcase our quality, and I made sure some large, well-known brands passed in front of the buyer during my sample show and tell.

I arrived on time and sat nervously in the lobby, mentally walking through my presentation.

When it was my time, I was ready. I went into the meeting room, sat down, and began to unpack the samples. I had brought a stinking library of samples. All the very best I could find. I had even raided my boss' secret stash to get some pristine samples we had produced recently.

I started my meeting by showing one incredible sample after another— color, graphics, die cuts, folding, cross overs, the best of the best. Even at my young age, I sensed the buyer was not impressed or he was simply bored. I was not sure, so I proceeded to talk, or show up and throw up, as all rookies do. I must have talked for twenty minutes, outlining the value of these beautiful samples and their well-known brand owners.

I am not sure when, but at some point, I realized I was doing all the talking. But, hey, that is what salespeople do, right? I kept right on going. After a good 30-40 minutes, I was really running out of things to say. All that time, the buyer had patiently been sitting and listening to my rambling.

Finally, he interrupted my spiel about quality, service, and samples. I will never forget what he said, and I quote:

> Greg, these are beautiful samples. But I fear I have wasted your time. You see, I do have a great need for printing and a great need for the best price and service I can obtain, but I only produce black-and-white printed manuals, journals, and books. I only have one full-color job all year, and it is our annual holiday Christmas card.

At this point, I quickly became aware that I had botched it. I thanked him for his time and made sure to tell him that if he ever had a need for more full-color printing, I would be happy to help. I then quickly packed up my volume of samples and returned to the office.

I never again received an opportunity with that account.

While driving back to the office, I left the radio completely off. I think better when there is total silence. My first thought was, "What will Bruce think?" Bruce was my boss and the company owner. He was so happy that my persistence had paid off and that I was really making headway with such a fantastic account.

A few days later, I sat in Bruce's office and, leaving out no details, I told him my sad story. I was sure there would definitely be some punishment handed out. To my surprise, Bruce simply sat, legs crossed, leaning slightly back in his chair, listening with that half smile on his face.

After I had laid out the disastrous meeting, Bruce stopped fidgeting with his glasses and said, "I am sorry to hear that, Greg, but I have to ask, do you know what went wrong here?"

"Well, yes," I said. "I was way off the mark. I didn't do my research or understand what this client really produces."

"No," said Bruce. "It's not about the research. It's about your behavior." And then he went on to impart some very valuable lessons:

1. Good sales representatives never assume.
2. Good sales representatives never do all the talking.
3. Good sales representatives must be great listeners.
4. Good sales representatives ask really good questions.
5. Good sales representatives always do their homework.
6. Good sales representatives never start selling until they figure out what the customer wants to buy.

Some lessons are painful but very educational. I can honestly say now, twenty-eight years later, I have rarely if ever made the same mistake. I now go to every first meeting with only a pen and pad for taking notes. Any samples come on follow-up visits.

How should you approach the first appointment with a new prospective customer? The meeting actually starts well before you even arrive, as we'll explore in the next section.

Pre-Call Planning

As with any meeting, it is important to take some time to plan out how you want the call to go. That said, most meetings rarely go exactly as planned. Nonetheless, you must do your best to sketch out what you want to achieve.

I once went to a meeting feeling pretty confident I could wing it. This was another situation where I learned a lesson the hard way. Back in 1994, just three years out of college and three years into my sales career, I was preparing for a presentation with a new prospective customer. Instead of doing my homework and preparing a nice presentation, I decided just to wing it. Why not? I had been in sales three years, and I was pretty confident about what I was doing, so I simply prepared my presentation for the buyer. To my surprise, not only did the buyer show up, but he brought his director of marketing and chief financial officer. They asked some really good questions, and most of them I could not answer. For example, when they asked who else in their industry I worked with, I was just not prepared, and it showed. It was an embarrassing situation, but I made sure it never happened again.

While the meeting can be a simple one-on-one, multiple people may also show up. Always assume others may show up to a meeting and prepare accordingly. For the purposes of this discussion, let's assume you are meeting with one person only.

It always pays to write down what your goals are for the meeting. Here are a few goals you may have:

1. Find some common ground between you and your customer.
2. Identify you are talking to the proper person.
3. Identify what motivates your new customer.
4. Confirm as many needs as you can in the limited time.
5. Create a bridge or a reason for the second meeting, if possible, with a larger audience.

There are three basic parts to the first meeting:

1. Introductions
2. Needs Analysis/Discussion
3. Conclusion

While these sound pretty simple, there is a lot going on here. Before we dive in and dissect the call, let me stress the importance of always taking notes during a meeting. First, it shows you are a professional, and second, it allows you to have all the details you need when reviewing the call.

We will talk further about the needs analysis and confirmed needs shortly, but I always want to understand a few things at every meeting, even if I fail to get a confirmed need. Following are questions

I always want to ask and understand:

1. Why did you call me? (assuming the customer called you)
2. What are the challenges/issues/problems?
3. What is your current situation?
4. Whom are you currently working with?
5. What are you currently paying?
6. What are your goals and objectives?

These are just some basic questions I like to understand because they usually relate to underlying needs if you drill down during the meeting.

Three Primary Meeting Stages

Meeting Stage 1: Introduction

You only get to make a first impression once, so you need to make a good one. Aside from the basics, such as being on time and dressing appropriately, you need to bring a level of confidence that shows you are comfortable meeting and interacting with new people.

The Power of Small Talk

When you first arrive, remember you are trying to make a friend, create a bond, or build rapport with the customer. Look around the room. Are your prospective customers into baseball? Do they have pictures of their children on their desks? Is there an obvious display of their favorite sports team? Are they neat and tidy, or is the office a mess? Scan the room like a detective to find something to use to generate small talk. Look for something you have in common. Never underestimate the power of small talk and bonding, as people like people who are like them.

Another way to establish a relationship is to focus more on "we" than "me." Too many young salespeople spend too much time saying *I* can do this, *I* can do that, *I* think, *I* know, etc. Remember, you are there to support and help your customer. This means you need to be focusing on the use of "we." Also, remember that "We" can be you and the customer, or "we" can be you and your team, but *we* is inclusive; *we* is a team; *we* has a win-win feel to it.

Equal Business Stature

It is also important to establish what is commonly called equal business stature. What this simply means is that your potential customer sees you as an equal and someone worthy of a business relationship. Your customer needs to know you are a professional, you know your stuff, and you are able to deliver what you promise. There are several ways to demonstrate this. The following examples assume a B2B situation.

1. Study and use industry terms from the customer's industry. Every industry has its own unique vocabulary. Understanding and using similar language goes a long way to establishing your credibility.

2. Look at what is going on in the customer's industry. Are there trends? Are there obvious issues and problems you can identify to show you understand the environment your customer operates in?

3. Try to identify what the business drivers are in the customer's business. In each industry (banking, construction, healthcare, etc.), there are different business drivers. Within each of these industries, each company may have similar, the same, or totally different business drivers. Understanding what drives business will be helpful later in the process, when you are constructing the proposal and building a business case.

4. As just mentioned, you must establish credibility. One way

to do this is to talk about similar customers you have worked with, the challenges faced, and the solutions you came up with.

5. Finally, use testimonials. It is one thing to talk about what you have done, but to get your other customers to provide testimonials about your work and the success you have had is helpful in having your customer see you as the right person for the job.

In the early stages of the meeting, you will have several goals.

1. Confirm you are meeting with the right person. I can't tell you how often salespeople start with the wrong person, fail to figure it out, and waste valuable time talking to the wrong person.

2. Ask who else is part of the decision-making process? On large ticket items or ongoing programs, there rarely is just one person who will make all the decisions. Never take a no from someone who can't say yes.

3. Assuming you are meeting with the proper person, you need to understand what type of person he or she is. There are two types of people, and I like to refer back to Tom Freese's definition of them in *Question Based Selling*: "While some people are motivated to run fast toward Gold Medals, many other people run even faster from German Shepherds." The goal is to identify what type of person you are talking with. Some are motivated by achieving success while others are motivated by not making a mistake. While it may not be easy to figure out which personality type you're meeting with, it's crucial to understand what motivates a person. This is not just something you do in the beginning of the meeting; rather it is something you do throughout the meeting, with good questions and good listening. Later, this knowledge will be indispensable in the needs analysis and proposal stage. It is critical to remember you are not selling yet.

Meeting Stage 2: Discussion/Needs Analysis

Most of the meeting will be the discussion/needs analysis, and it will make or break the meeting. It is important to understand the primary goal of the meeting, in general, is to identify and confirm your customer's needs. Not what needs you think your customer has, but actual needs. There is *no* guessing here. This is called a needs analysis, and it is performed by asking good questions, listening, asking more good questions, and taking good notes. It is important to remember you are not selling yet; you are identifying your customer's needs, goals, pain and objectives, so you can eventually prepare a relevant and on-target proposal.

Before each meeting, you should always try to figure out what needs you think the customer may have based on what you know. When you get to the meeting, you are essentially looking for a good fit. In the meeting, you can probe and confirm the needs, or you may find your assumptions were not correct and you have uncovered needs you were not expecting. Asking good questions is the key to understanding your customer and what you can do to help. The key here is to get the customer talking. If you ask the proper questions and don't interrupt, most customers will start talking, provide useful information, and in most cases, lead to your next good question. If you are not patient or keep interrupting, you can slow this process.

Here's an example about assumptions. In my print sales business, I assume my customers are all looking for the best price, best quality, and fastest turn-around time. In my line of work, these are safe assumptions, but not always the most important or only needs a customer has. Needs such as speed to market, waste, obsolescence, distribution… and many more can be just as important.

During the needs analysis phase of the discussion, what questions will you ask to try to determine your customer's most important needs? It would be nice if you could simply ask what your customer needed, but in many situations, the customer may not know the true needs, and you can help figure it out. For example, if a customer is looking for the best price, quality, and turn-around time, which one is the most important? If your proposal is the lowest cost, but delivers late, is that okay? If the proposal offers the best quality, but the highest cost, is that okay? Helping a customer list and prioritize needs, as well as helping to uncover some the customer was not aware of is powerful.

I once heard that most customers know 80 percent of the problems their companies have. As an example, keeping costs low is typically a problem most businesses face, and most business owners would agree lowering costs is good and always a need in business.

Keep in mind that if your prospective customer manufacturers a product and thinks his material costs are too high, that is an opportunity for you, but it's also an opportunity for every other salesperson talking to this particular client. Every manufacturer who sources materials to build a product will probably tell you that his material costs are too high. What if you not only talked about the obvious problems like high costs, but you also talked about the other 20 percent of problems your customer may not realize exist. In this same example of keeping costs low, your competition might simply try to sell products/services at a lower price to solve this problem. What if you asked better questions than your competition and found out that your customer had a waste or obsolescence problem that added unnecessary cost to the business? What if one of the benefits of your solution could solve this problem, and as a result, it would lower the costs? What if the waste and obsolescence problem had a value far greater than your solution? Can you imagine if the particular product you are trying to sell costs the customer $20,000, but solves a problem costing the customer $50,000, $100,000, or more? I once heard a saying, "People only spend big money to solve big problems."

I believe in addressing the 80 percent of obvious, known problems.

But I think those who really want to deliver the home run should shine a light on the 20 percent of problems a customer isn't addressing. This can only be done by asking good questions and listening.

Unfortunately, not all questions are created equal. Try to always ask open-ended questions. Open-ended questions are designed to avoid a one-word response. For example, someone asks you if you liked a particular movie and you say "Yes." Or they could say, "Tell me what you liked about the movie…." As you can see, with an open-ended question, it is pretty hard to give a one-word answer. Here are a few open-ended questions to try to get the customer talking so you can uncover the true needs.

Price:

- Tell me about where you sell your product?
- Who are your direct competitors and how many do you have?
- What is unique about your product?
- How does our price to you affect your price to your customer?

Quality:

- What brand standards for printed literature do your vendors need to follow?
- Tell me about your company quality control requirements?
- What are typical problems you see on your projects today?

Time:

- How do you get your products to market?
- How do trade shows play a part in your marketing efforts?
- How many new products do you bring to market each year?
- How does a late delivery affect you financially?

Note: When working in a B2B environment, it is always a good idea to think of the questions you are asking in terms of your customers' experience and their customers' experience. If you can have a positive impact on both customers' experiences, that is huge.

Most of these questions are designed to get the customer talking, and that is a good thing, as long as you are listening and taking notes. Each one of these questions can generate additional questions if you are listening. For example, if the customer says she really doesn't have any competitors, you may want to get her to explain the situation. If she truly has no competitors, then price may not be the biggest need. Conversely, if a customer says she has lots of competitors and sells primarily at trade shows, then you can probe the needs she may have for best pricing and on-time delivery. The average trade show lasts two to three days. If you are three days late, that is a big problem. Remember, you are still not selling; you are looking for what your customer really needs, or ultimately, what the customer wants to buy. If you uncover an interesting item in your questioning, do not be afraid to drill down. For example, if customers say their last vendor was late with delivery (or the quality was not what they expected, etc.), drill down and ask, "How does late delivery affect your business?" Then let them share their pain with you. When customers share and talk about pain out loud, this reinforces why they are talking to you—to alleviate pain. This is powerful. People spend money to solve problems, and pain indicates a problem.

As you progress through the meeting, you are like a sponge soaking up everything you hear, asking good questions, observing the answers, and if they generate follow-up questions, asking those questions. There is a process for drilling down that looks something like this.

Q: What turn-around time do you require?

A: Six days.

Q: What happens if your vendor delivers in seven days?

A: That is a huge problem, since we deliver directly to trade shows that last only two days.

Q: What happens if a shipment misses the trade show dates?

A: First, I will get in big trouble. My boss will be all over me, and I might even lose my job. Second, what we sell at the trade show is just the introductory product. This product creates more money later in the year based on reorders. We have calculated that missing one day at a trade show equals up to $50,000 in lost revenue later in the year.

Q: What would happen if your partner delivered on time but the quality was not great?

A: Well, most of what we produce is not full color or critical color; it is mainly black and white literature and user manuals, so even if it is not at our quality expectations, it is still better to have the materials on time, as is, than to miss the show completely.

Q: So it is fair to say that being on time is mission critical?

A: Yes, on-time delivery is all that matters in our business. We have spent a lot of money overnighting products to ensure we do not miss out on any days at the trade shows.

Q: Would it be fair to say if a partner can't, or is not sure it can, deliver in six days, that nothing else matters?

A: Yes, that is the starting point for all discussion. If you cannot deliver on time, there is nothing else to talk about.

As you can see, first asking some fact questions, such as how many days the customer requires for turn time, then walking through why it is a problem, and then letting the customer tell you about the pain helps the customer feel the pain he experiences when things do not go well. Also, let the customer explain how this pain impacts business and who suffers as a result, and finally, get confirmation that being on time with a six-day turn is indeed the prima-ry need. I can't overstate the importance of letting customers talk about their pain.

In a nutshell, if you identify pain, ask the customer to describe the pain, ask the customer what this pain does to business, and then ask what it would be like not to have this pain, you will have the information you need to provide a compelling proposal.

This is just one confirmed need. Throughout the entire meeting, you are probing in different directions to try to uncover as many confirmed needs as possible. If you can pull out one, two, or even three confirmed needs, you are doing well. You may find your as-sumptions are correct, or you may find additional needs you did not foresee. Remember, you are not selling yet; you are still gath-ering information.

Business Drivers

I think this may be a good time to introduce you to the concept of a business driver. For those of you selling B2B, it is important to understand what a business driver is and how it can help you in your sales efforts. Business drivers are anything that has an impact on a company's growth and profitability. Processes, resources, and people who aid in bringing in revenue and growing a business are all important.

Two types of business drivers exist: internal and external. Internal drivers are within each company. A good example is a salesperson, or a sales process that helps the company bring in revenue and grow. Internal drivers are easy to control and modify as needed.

An external driver is outside the company and can be much more difficult to control. Common external business drivers are legisla-tion or trade policies, and customer activities that can either help or hurt your business.

Many businesses in the same industry, like banks or insurance companies, may have similar business drivers, but honestly, all businesses have different business drivers. The reason is each business defines differently what makes it successful. One bank may list its bank tellers as one of its primary business drivers because they help open new accounts and sell ancillary services to customers who are at their windows. Other banks may have a more online focus and consider online advertising as their main business driver.

Regardless of what the business driver is, I always recommend figuring out what each customer's business driver is. This can be done by simply asking good questions about how his business works or how it is set up. If, for example, your customer has his own outside sales force, it is pretty safe to assume his salespeople are a business driver. Once you know what the business drivers are, it makes it much easier to identify your customer's needs. Look for needs that impact a company's business drivers.

When a Confirmed Need Is also a Business Driver

Confirming needs is the goal; however, the holy grail of a confirmed need is when a confirmed need is also a business driver or substantially impacts a business driver for your client.

For example, if in your discussions, you figure out that one of your customer's business drivers is his sales force and you also confirm that getting sales literature into the hands of his sales team is a confirmed need, you have hit on a golden opportunity.

If the outside sales force is one of your customer's primary drivers of revenue, and one of the confirmed needs is to get literature produced and in the sales team's hands, then all you have to do is ask what it costs the company per day if its team is not out in the field selling with literature. You will get a number. This number is to be used in a future business case or in a discussion about risk.

I was once doing my needs analysis for a Seattle company that produced cranes and heavy machinery. Each one of these machines had literature, like an owner's manual, safety stickers, and warranty information that was paired up with the machine on the production line. In probing, I found out that when the literature was late, it actually stopped the line. Their entire manufacturing process was based on building the machine and pairing the accompanying literature on the line simultaneously. When the line stopped due to late delivery of literature, it cost $9,000 per hour. As you can imagine, it is not hard to use this $9,000 per hour information to build a business case for on-time delivery later in the proposal.

You will notice I keep saying "You are not selling yet." The key is not to start selling too early. As explained earlier, if you start selling too early, this is what we call *show up and throw up.* This is common for new, inexperienced salespeople who don't know that listening and asking good questions is how you gather information and eventually create a relevant, on-target proposal down the road. If you start selling before you fully understand your customer's needs, you may be selling him on the lowest cost when what he really needs is a guaranteed production plan for a certain number of days. You will use these needs in your proposal at a later date.

Also, keep in mind, depending on the complexity of the sale and type of industry, I have literally sat through three two-hour meetings on three different days, gathering information, confirming needs, and fully understanding a customer's business before I even start building a proposal.

Asking Good Questions

The following story illustrates the power of asking good questions.

Seattle-Based HMO

Early in my career, after a few futile attempts to contact the buyer at a large HMO, I finally got an opportunity to provide a proposal.

It was a proposal for a drug formulary for about $17,000. Back in 1996, that was a pretty good-sized order, not to mention it was black and white printing, which means it was far less effort than a similar job with full color.

As soon as I had my proposal ready, I called Dave (the customer), told him I would be in downtown Seattle, and asked if I could stop by to drop off my proposal. He said, "Sure, as long as you are in the area, feel free to stop by." I wasn't really in the area, but I wanted to deliver my proposal in person.

I arrived and did my standard spiel: Here is my proposal, here are the specs as I understood them, here is the price, and so on. I mentioned that one of the things we are good at is price, quality, and service. I also mentioned that we guarantee delivery on or before the day agreed upon.

Dave simply sat and listened. I feared he was bored and I might be losing the sale. He really expressed no emotions, so I could not tell what he was thinking. So, like any newbie, I just kept talking.

Finally, I was finished. He still had not said one word. I sat there for what seemed like a week as he reviewed my proposal. He then opened a file on his desk and pulled out another piece of paper that was undoubtedly a comparison proposal. After comparing the two, he looked at me and said, "Greg, your price of $17,000 is about $7,000 higher than my other price." And then, silence. He simply awaited my response.

Now, this to me is where a sales professional earns his or her money. There are many ways to respond to the situation but nearly all will not help. I could have said:

1. "Where do you need me to be on price?"
2. "I guess that means I lose" (and hightail it out of there!)
3. "I can take this back to my boss to see what we can do; do you have a target price?"

To me, all those things seemed a bit off the mark. Overcoming a 41 percent deficit is pretty impossible. Fortunately for me, I was new, and too stupid to know I was beat. I decided to ask a question. It is dumb luck that I happened to come up with the right question, and to this day, I am not sure where it came from, but it was a very big aha moment for me in my sales career.

While Dave sat and waited for my response, I simply said, "So, what does that mean?"

Dave looked at me, looked back at my proposal, then looked up and said, "That means you damn well better not be late." Then, he looked over at the corner of his desk and nodded. There sat a pile of film—we used film in those days. He said, "Take the film, and you better have my project delivered on the fifteenth—no excuses."

Now, I was new, but I was not completely stupid. I had learned a long time ago to shut up, grab the film, and get the heck out of that office. Anything I said after that would have only served to increase the risk of Dave changing his mind, and I knew it.

I drove back to my office. I was so nervous, I could barely drive. Why had he given me this job when I was arguably the highest price? Was it a trick? It was too easy. Well, when I got back to the office and told the story to my team, everyone was amazed. I was still baffled about why. It was then that my boss, Bruce Walker, spoke up and put in his word of wisdom. He said, "Someday you will find out. It is my guess that you provided something no one else provided, something more valuable than money or at least more valuable than $7,000. Never forget, not everyone is simply after the low bid." Then, as usual, he slowly walked away.

I was still determined to find out why.

That year ended, and by the time the sales for this HMO were all tallied up, I had produced nearly one million dollars of black-and-white printing for Dave. Once again, one million dollars of black-

and-white printing is a lot of printing. After about three months, I finally summoned the courage to ask Dave why he had chosen me, the new guy, and the high-priced guy, for that very first job.

"First," he explained, "you delivered your proposal in person. I knew you were probably just coming to Seattle to see me and the thirty-mile drive was a sign of your commitment—all the other proposals were simply faxed in. Second, you guaranteed your delivery. I'm not sure how you knew it, but on-time delivery is the key to success at my job. The HMO is required by federal law to get the formulary published by a certain date. Every day that material is not available, we're fined $1,000 a day until delivered. The last low-priced printers I used were low bidders. But one was late by three days and one was late by seven days. So, as you can see, the low bidders were now the high bidders, and my boss was all over my ass for going over budget and being late.

"So, why did I pick you? Well, here is a list of the problems you solved for me:

1. You delivered your proposal in person. You explained your proposal and looked for anything that could cause problems. This gave me confidence.
2. You guaranteed your delivery, and you made it happen.
3. Because you made it happen, we were not fined for the first time in three printings.
4. Because you made it happen, my boss had no reason to yell at me for cost overruns.
5. Because you made it happen, my boss had no reason even to come talk to me.
6. Essentially, you reduced my risk and kept me off my boss's radar."

Once again, it was a very big aha moment for me. Here's what I learned:

1. Face to face is the best way to sell.
2. Be bold. Try to come up with an educated guess about what is

valuable to your client. Then confirm what is really important to him or her.

3. Low price is not the only criteria; if it is, you probably have not yet uncovered the right needs/pain points.
4. Never underestimate the power of asking good questions.
5. Not all questions are equal.

Selling Too Early in the Process

The Order of Operations

In sales, there is an order of operations that will lead to greater success. Remember back in middle school when you learned about the "Order of Operations" in math class? Simply stated, when you approach a math problem, you have a step-by-step process you go through in a particular order to get the right answer. Another example would be your driver's license test. First, you get your learner's permit; then you practice driving; then you study for the written exam, and once you pass your written exam, you take the driving test and voilà, you obtain your license. You must go through this process in this order. Can you imagine what would happen if you skipped the practice driving, did not study, and jumped right to the written/driving test? It would not be pretty, and you would probably not get the result you were looking for.

The sales process also has an order of operations, so this entire book has been written in the sales operations sequence. The difference in sales is that you could do some of the steps out of order and still win, but you are lowering your odds of success. Often, if you lose, it is best to go back to see if or where you missed a step. The problem comes when you cannot identify why you lost. This is why selling too early in the process can be dangerous. You may be selling a car when your customer is looking to buy a truck. If you skip a step, you may simply assume the price of your car was too high and not really understand that your price was fine; your car just can't haul gravel very well, and that is a need you missed early on in the process.

Nothing guarantees success in sales, but if at every step you are increasing your odds of success, it stands to reason you are lowering the odds of failure by the same amount.

As I write this, I am compelled to tell a story from just last week. I had a new paper merchant reach out to me with a new, unique paper that was made out of stone, not tree pulp. Naturally, I was intrigued, so I went to the meeting.

The CEO and his small team of three support folks came to the meeting, and they proceeded to talk and talk and talk.

They told me the paper was recyclable, not recycled. They told me it was priced less than other synthetic sheets. They told me they keep 34" rolls on hand locally, but other sizes needed to be special ordered. As you can see, they just kept talking.

One interesting part of the meeting was that they talked a different language. They talked about their paper thickness in terms of microns, but in printing, we talk in terms of pounds. In printing, we use standard-sized rolls that are 35", but they had 34" rolls on hand. Note: In printing, 35" rolls are the minimum to create the standard 8.5" x 11" sizes.

Not once did these salespeople ask me about my customers, what my customers needed, or what I thought of their paper. Not once did they ask questions, any questions, much less pay attention to my answers.

Their behavior was the opposite of professional selling, so I was pretty shocked. In short, they were selling way too early. In fact, they were selling something I was not buying, but they did not know this.

It is critical to remember, if you are selling too early, there is a good chance you will be selling something your customer is not looking to buy. You must walk through the process far enough to understand what your customer needs. While this is helpful in transactional selling, it is especially true if you are selling ongoing program-type products. Transactional sales are simply individual jobs or project sales. Program sales are where you have an ongoing program year round where you are continuously supplying product to your customer.

Early in my career, I was trained to be what is called a transactional sales representative. This is not bad, but as in life, things change and you must adapt. Later in my career, I decided that while this approach does work, it limits me to small transactions, so I have to keep scurrying around for every little job I can get my hands on. In short, it was not the best use of my time.

Fortunately, in this position I met one of my great friends and mentors, Catherine McGavin. In my opinion, this woman missed her true calling. While she can sell and she can sell big, she is a natural teacher. Catherine was hired at my company to do two things: 1) Bring her consultative sales approach with her to land large program-based accounts, and 2) Share her approach with others on our sales team.

I quickly recognized I needed this skill set, so I started what I like to call my second career in sales. While painful, it was and is still well worth the effort. I say "is" because I am still learning. I learn something new just about every day.

First, let's clarify what is meant by these two different types of selling:

Transactional Selling: In printing, if your customer calls and asks for a proposal, you provide it, you win it, you deliver it, you invoice for it, and then you are done with the project and wait for the next one, you are probably a transactional salesperson. You may have two or two hundred different projects during the year, but you are a transactional salesperson.

Consultative/Program Selling: In printing, if you call your customer and ask for a meeting to explore his needs, better understand his processes, understand how he makes money, and what is important to him, and then, with this knowledge, show him how he can take the two hundred jobs he currently sends you, and put together an inventory solution, just-in-time solution, print-on-demand solution, or paper program using common paper to reduce paper costs and increase brand consistency, you are a consultative salesperson. This approach is more "program-focused" than "job-focused."

In my opinion, there are times for both. If given the opportunity to sell a job or sell an account, I choose the account every time.

As a consultative salesperson, your job is to identify and understand the customer's true needs and sell to those needs. Sure, every buyer wants the best price, a quick turnaround, good service, and great quality—heck, anyone can figure that out. However, what about waste, obsolescence, time to market, nimbleness, return on investment, and disaster recovery? These are all concerns that have a dollar value to your customer. If you cannot pull out what is important to your customer, you will be selling too early or selling something your customer is not buying.

How Not to Sell Too Early

One of my first experiences with consultative selling was with Catherine McGavin when I tried to get the business of a seminar training company.

This training company was based in Bellevue, Washington, and it created training manuals for its seminars. The company had an approximate print budget of one million dollars, so it was a sizable account, producing thirty manuals for each seminar, depending on attendance, which it shipped to more than 2,600 locations across the United States

First, I called this business. The person I spoke to told me the company was buying its training manuals very efficiently and did not see the need to talk to me. I got a little bold and said if I did not think I could show the company something different, I would not be calling. This worked and I got an appointment. I was told the company representative could only spare an hour. I said, "No problem." I can do a lot in an hour.

Excitedly, I called my mentor Catherine to tell her what I was doing. She said it would be a great opportunity to start learning the consultative sales approach. I agreed, so she and I sat down to plan out the meeting.

Here is where the pain starts. When you are a transactional salesperson, you simply want to show up, get the specs to bid on, win the work, and get your commission. As I was to learn, that was not how this meeting was going to play out.

Catherine asked me what I knew about this account. I laid out the information above. She then asked what I wanted to get or learn on the first meeting. "First meeting?" I asked. She said, "Yes. To learn all we need to learn and perform a true needs analysis, we will most likely have two or three meetings." My head was spinning. "But he promised me one hour of his time," I replied. She told me we had just identified our first goal for the meeting. After one hour, he must want us to come back for a second meeting. "Oh, brother" was all I was thinking.

Once again, Catherine was correct. We proceeded to work through three meetings in total, uncovering countless needs, goals, pain, and objectives. In the end, our printing price was on par with the customer's current printer, but our solution, when understood in its entirety, saved the customer nearly $200,000. It had less to do with actual printing costs, and more to do with three full-time employees the company did not need, in a warehouse it did not need, shipping orders across the country, which it did not need to do.

This type of solution can only be accomplished by asking good questions, listening, and taking good notes.

Taking Notes

At this time, I would like to carve out a few comments on taking notes. We are all busy and have many things on our minds. We have multiple meetings every day, and multiple customers, so committing everything to memory is a terribly risky and, honestly, silly thing to do.

I cannot tell you how many times young salespeople sit through an entire meeting and have a conversation, but never pull out the pen and paper to take notes. Then they struggle in the car or back at the office to recreate notes after the meeting. I cannot reiterate enough how important it is to take notes for every meeting in real time.

I often make notes in an outline format prior to the meeting. I write down the needs I am assuming exist, I write down what I would like to know from this meeting, and I simply check them off as we progress.

I also create new notes based on where the question and answers take the meeting. If, during the meeting, you reconfirm a need, write it down, and circle it. Only circle the confirmed needs, but make sure you note all important aspects of the meeting. So why take notes? For several reasons:

1. **Taking notes looks professional.** When you take notes properly, your customers feel you are really listening and paying attention.

2. **Taking notes makes you more accurate.** If you need to report to a sales manager or your boss and she asks you to write up a post-call summary, you are nearly done and you are accurate. You are not frantically trying to recreate facts and figures. If you do not report to anyone, it is still a good idea to have extremely accurate notes so that eventually you can build a proposal with confidence that you are addressing the customer's needs exactly.

3. **Taking notes helps you remember who was in the meeting.** Often, more than one person will be meeting with you. Make sure to write down who was in the meeting and each person's respective role.

4. **Taking notes gives you a checklist.** If you employ the pre-meeting notes like I do, you have a checklist to work from. Toward the end of the meeting, it is not uncommon for your prospective customer to ask if there is anything else you would like to know. Customers understand that to provide a proposal, you need information. At this point, simply check your notes. Any item on your list that is important and has not yet been addressed can quickly be addressed.

5. **Data for CRM:** At some point if you install a CRM system, having good notes makes it easy to keep track of all your sales activity so you are organized and can keep you efforts progressing.

Meeting Stage 3: Conclusion/Leaving Bridge

As you can see, you first had the introduction and created rapport with your potential new customer. Then you walked through the discussion portion of the meeting, where you spent time confirming your client's needs, goals, pain, and objectives to ensure you are fully prepared to create a compelling proposal that meets the stated needs.

How do you end the meeting? Keep in mind, depending on the complexity of you solution, it is not unheard of to have several meetings to get all the information you need to prepare a compelling and relevant proposal and/or presentation.

That said, you should always end a meeting with three things in mind:

1. **Summarize:** Always take the time to review what was just dis-

cussed, confirm the major points, and paint a picture. Also, when you do uncover a need, confirm the need by restating the need to make sure it is a real need and that you understand the need.

2. **Paint a picture:** I find it best to try to paint a picture of what could be. It is important at a very high level to summarize and walk through the meeting, using your notes to paint a picture of what your future proposal will contain. Again, you must have good notes, and you must feel comfortable that you have identified true needs. For example, you could wrap up by asking what it would look like if you could lower the customer's costs, improve its quality, and reduce its customer complaints. Keep in mind, and this is important, that this wrap-up assumes you have identified that lowering costs, achieving better quality, and reducing customer complaints are truly problems your customer needs to solve.

3. **Leave a bridge:** Always leave a bridge to the next meeting. Try to line up the next-in person visit before you leave. If all that is needed to generate a winning proposal is one meeting, then arrange a follow-up meeting to make a presentation. Simply faxing or emailing a proposal can work, but remember, your odds always go up if you are face-to-face with your customer.

If your situation calls for more than one meeting, then the bridge is more of a natural step in the process. Often, a prospective customer will agree to meet with you to see if you have a serious solution to share. If you do, the customer may want to call a meeting with additional stakeholders in the company to share the opportunity further.

One great way to keep in contact and strengthen the relationship is to arrange a tour. There are two types of tours.

1. Invite the customer to take a tour of your location if your solution or product is made at a physical location. Getting a tour and

seeing how his product will be made is a way to bond and help your client get a better picture of how you will actually do what you say you will do. This can be very powerful.

2. Ask to take a tour of the customer's location to see how your customer will use the solution or product in the real world. This can be an enormous help in identifying needs and issues with a current process. Sometimes, fresh eyes see things from an outside perspective that others miss. A tour is an opportunity to really get inside your customer's operation and start thinking from their perspective about what would really be helpful.

So why is leaving a bridge important? My research has led me to believe that around 40 percent of prospects become customers when the process is face-to-face compared with approximately a 16 percent success rate for business done over the phone or via email. Regardless of the numbers, face-to-face is much more effective.

Never forget that every time you get face-to-face, that is a touchpoint. If part of the process is developing rapport and creating a bond with a customer, there is no better way than in person.

If you are looking to grow your business, you should always defer to the process that reduces your odds of losing and increases your odds of winning at every turn. If the odds are in your favor, you will eventually get where you need to be.

Practice

Those who know me understand that soccer has always been my favorite sport. I played up until I was forty-eight and I coached for nearly fifteen years. The one thing soccer and sales have in common is the need to practice.

In every meeting, at some point your customers will ask you to tell them about your company, so you had better be prepared to walk them through an organized, thoughtful, and brief overview about yourself and your business. Remember, as a small business owner, you are your business and you will always be a "unique" characteristic of your business, so don't be afraid to tailor your overview about you and your business. Personalizing the description of your business helps people understand the value you provide.

Since I am not a fan of a show up and throw up mentality or the salesperson doing all the talking, I do a lot of listening, but customers will want you to share at some point. Before I go to a meeting, I walk through my mini-presentation many, many times to ensure I can almost do it in my sleep. The good news is that once you have done this, you can repurpose it for any meeting, but you need to have practiced long before you set foot in the meeting.

Summary

In this chapter, we walked through the anatomy of your first appointment with a new customer. It is important to remember the order of operations or the proper order of how the meeting should proceed. No meeting ever goes exactly to plan, but at least having a plan will give you the best chance of success. As discussed, many sales systems/methodologies exist that you can use in a meeting, so pick one that works for you. The key is to uncover needs in the meeting, so however you do it is fine. Having a sales methodology when you are in the appointment allows you to avoid the dreaded show up and throw up scenario. Also, never forget the value of pre-call planning so you are clear on what you want to accomplish in the meeting. As they say, "If you have no map, any road will do." And "any road" is not usually the best plan. Remember there are three primary stages to every meeting: 1) the introduction and small talk to try to bond with your prospective customer, 2) the needs analysis where you are looking to uncover confirmed needs and understand business drivers by asking good questions, listening, and taking good notes, and 3) the conclusion where you restate what needs you have uncovered and leave a bridge for the next step in the process. In the next chapter, we will dive into what to do with all the information you have gathered. We will talk about the proposal and executing the sale.

Exercise

1. With a friend, create a mock meeting and role-play. This can be one way to practice walking through a meeting.

    _____

    _____

    _____

    _____

2. Look up and research which sales system/methodology you feel is the best fit for you. Now go buy the book and study.

    _____

    _____

    _____

    _____

3. To practice pre-call planning, list the things you think you might want to know in a first meeting. If the list is more than five, pick the five most important.

    _____

    _____

    _____

    _____

4. Make a commitment to look at your top customers and figure out what the business drivers are in those industries.

_____

_____

_____

_____

5. Make a list of some good open-ended questions that could be used in any meeting.

_____

_____

_____

_____

6. Make a list of what type of "bridge" is most appropriate for your business (follow-up appointment, phone call, tour, etc.).

_____

_____

_____

_____

CHAPTER 8
EXECUTING THE SALE

The Proposal

Almost time to start selling. Once you have worked through the process and you feel you have identified and confirmed your potential customer's need, goals, pain, and objectives, it is time to move to the next phase: putting it all together in the form of a proposal. This is a critical step in the sales process. You will see how good your notes are, how accurate your needs analysis was, and most of all, you may start facing objections. Here is where selling really starts, so let's get to it.

Getting Organized

Do you have all you need? The first thing you need to do is make sure you are organized. You have spent what may be a lot of time and effort already, so you need to ensure you have what you need to create a proposal. This is where you put it all together. Earlier in this book we talked about the questions "Do you have a product?" and "What is unique about your product?" and we did a whole lot of upstream work to get ready for this stage.

Have you done your homework? If you are missing any critical information, find a way to get it before you prepare the proposal. At this point, one missing piece of information could destroy your chance for success. Remember, there are many steps to this process. If you get to the very end of your presentation and the prospective client simply says that your price is too high, then you probably missed something along the way. During the process, you usually uncover enough information to know if you are the right fit for the job at hand, and you usually know if you are competing against the usual suspects.

Back in 2011, I was working on a very large program proposal for a major big-box retailer based in Issaquah, Washington. The annual value was approximately a million dollars, and because it was a two- to three-year contract, it was a substantial opportunity. I spent a good eight months working on this project, including several weeks spent collecting data and then flying the customer's senior management team into Medford, Oregon, to take a tour and walk through an overview of the workflow we were proposing. We spent the next few weeks constructing a preliminary pricing proposal. In the final few months, the customer wanted to understand better how our proprietary technology system worked, so we let them know that before we could get to that point, we would need to have a deal inked, a letter of intent, or a deposit against the implementation costs that would be required. To our surprise, the customer provided a $50,000 deposit, with $25,000 upfront, and the balance due when we finished the implementation. Wow, we were ecstatic! My boss was in that meeting, and he was jumping for joy. On the way home, he kept telling me, "You did it! You got this one." While I was trying to be positive, my gut was telling me not to celebrate too early.

It turned out that I was right to trust my gut. Within a few weeks of the deposit, we received the call that the company was going in a different direction. When I asked why, I was told our price was too high. In the eight-month process, we had provided our pricing in the second month, so the customer had our pricing very early on. If pricing was the real issue, wouldn't we have known before then? Why did we get to the end of the eight-month process before we found out our price was too high?

Lesson Learned: Always gain pricing agreement early on. Then you can iron out other details.

Years later, I would find out the real reason the customer left. It was a risk issue. In our proposal, we had a non-compete clause from another customer that did not allow us to manufacture in our existing Medford, Oregon, facility. In our proposal, we outlined our plan to develop a new plant in Seattle, closer to the customer. In actuality, all we were going to do was create space in our Seattle manufacturing facility for the equipment needed to produce the product. While this would not be as time-consuming as building a new building, it was risky because the peak season was just around the corner. In hindsight, this was a huge risk for our customer, so we should have focused more on it and investigated it further. The customer wanted to be complete in August, live end-to-end testing in September, and ready to launch live with its consumers on October 1. That only left two months for us to build-out the site. A build like this takes time to set up and time to run end-to-end testing before it goes live. While possible, a typical build like this takes about two to three months, if all goes well. In short, our customer could possibly put its customers at risk if we were not ready in time. The fact that this program generated nearly 85 percent of its annual revenue from October to November made us a huge risk for them.

Our competitor was up and running, and from what I heard, spent a lot of time talking about the challenges with starting up a new site from scratch. In the end, we were the riskier option.

Could we have approached the situation differently? Yes. Would we have won? I would like to say, yes, we would have won. To this day, I feel we were winning right up until we missed a major need, the need not to put our client's customers at risk of failure.

Once you are sure you are not missing anything and have what you need, it is time to start constructing the proposal.

Building a Relevant Proposal

Why do I say "building a *relevant* proposal" and not simply "building a proposal"? It's simple. If you build a world-class proposal based on providing the best pricing and quality, and the customer is actually looking to buy fastest turn-around time and guaranteed delivery date, you will see the customer is not buying what you are selling. To be relevant, you must be selling what the customer is looking to buy. You can have the best price and best quality, and still lose if the customer's true needs are simply turn time and guaranteed delivery. This is why the need analysis is so important.

Who Is Your Audience?

For whom are you writing the proposal? Again, for the sake of this discussion, I'm assuming we're in a B2B environment. Regardless of whom you write the proposal for, write it as if someone else in the organization will eventually read it. Sure, you may be talking to a group of people, and after a long process, they should all know a lot about you, your solution, and your company. But what if, behind the scenes, they run the proposal by the CFO, CEO, or even an owner? These people will eventually be directly involved in the decision, but they may not be involved in the upfront discussion, so if the proposal was written only for those who already know you, you may lose the new person who was brought in for final review. If this is the CFO, CEO, or CMO, this is a problem. Always write your proposal as if those reading it do not yet know everything about you.

What Format Will You Use?

The bottom line is to use the best format to convey your proposal to your audience. Formats can take many shapes, but they should all contain some very similar sections.

- **Introduction:** Greeting and setting the stage for the proposal to follow.

- **Experience/Credibility:** Establish your experience and why you are uniquely qualified to provide the following solution.

- **Restate the problems/confirmed needs:** Walk through the confirmed needs and associated pain you are addressing.

- **Spell out the solution:** Articulate the features and benefits of your solution. Never forget to build a case for doing business with you if you have math to support it. Use any quantifiable math to provide a compelling reason for your solution.

- **Paint a picture using your solution:** Summarize the solution, what problem it solves, and how it meets the customer's needs. Paint a picture of what life will be like after your solution is in place.

- **Feedback:** Look for opportunities to have the customer interact during this process. You can and will still find new information at this stage that may benefit you.

You must not overlook the power of a quantifiable business case when creating your proposal. Again, let's revisit the training company example I gave earlier. I approached this training company in Bellevue, Washington, to see if I could print its manuals for the training seminars it did all over the country. It said sure, but that no one could match the price it was currently getting. Its local vendor printed all its manuals at a very low cost. The manuals were then delivered to the training company's warehouse, where the warehouse workers would insert some literature with each book and ship them out, in bulk, nationwide. Keep in mind this is a pretty typical model. Local printer delivers to a local warehouse, then the product gets shipped out to a final destination, which, in this case, was all over the United States.

As previously described, we had long meetings with this company, and through some very good question-and-answer sessions, I came up with a solution. While the current solution used one printing company, my company had seventy different printing locations around the nation, so I took a different approach. I quantified how much the company spent in ground shipping and some overnight shipping for those last-minute rushes. I also quantified how much money the prospective customer spent at seminar destinations doing last minute, quick printing to produce a few extra manuals for late arriving participants. I found that my prospect had two full-time employees and a lease payment for the warehouse where it received the manuals, then shipped them out. As you can imagine, that was a pretty large number when all wrapped up—about $200,000 annually.

My solution did several things. First, I used facilities closer to the final destination to produce the manuals. This removed the need for a warehouse lease payment, the need for two full-time employees, and drastically reduced the ground and overnight freight costs for shipping manuals all over the country.

The customer was currently spending about $1 million annually to create their manuals. My cost to produce the manuals came in just a little higher at about $1,050,000—about $50,000 more than the company was currently paying. However, my solution saved the company nearly $200,000 in other areas of its supply chain, so, overall, I saved them $150,000. As I mentioned earlier, tying a need to a business driver can create a home run. Having manuals in hand at the seminar was a need and a significant business driver.

While my customer did *need* to get the lowest cost to print their manuals, they were not aware that they also had a need to reduce freight costs, reduce its warehouse overhead, and reduce employee headcount. You don't need to be a math wizard to see that quantifying needs and using this information in your proposal is critically important and helps secure deals.

As discussed in Chapter 7, this is the 80/20 percent rule in action. Identifying and shedding a light on problems your customer may not be aware of can be quite powerful, and in some cases, it can take the pricing discussion out of the mix. Again, if you are selling a solution that costs $20,000 but solves a $100,000 problem, most will tend to focus on the $100,000 savings as opposed to the $20,000 cost.

How to Deliver the Proposal

I personally believe today's salespeople are getting lazy. They are opting for the fast, less personal approach of simply submitting proposals remotely over fax or email. As I write this, I use both fax and email, but honestly, I am really talking about email. Sure, webinars and other online virtual presentations exist; however, nothing is as good as the opportunity to present face-to-face.

Keep in mind that not every sales presentation must be in person, and not every business and/or product requires an in-person proposal and presentation. You simply must use common sense based on your product, services, and business model. However, for large ticket items, complex solutions, custom solutions, or on-going services, face-to-face is always the best way to improve your odds of winning.

There are several reasons for face-to-face presentations:

1. You took the time to make a presentation. This is appreciated by your prospective customer.

2. It can set you apart from your competition. Not everyone will do one so you will stand out.
3. You are still able to sell after your competitors have stopped.
4. You may face objections in the presentation that you can address in the moment.
5. Face-to-face is one more touchpoint. If you are trying to build rapport, you are getting more face time than your competition.
6. You can read the room. There is still time to tailor your presentation if you notice something is not resonating.
7. You have the opportunity to ask for the order. It is easier to say no to an email than it is to someone's face.

The Power of No, a Polite No

Many people, both in and outside of sales, hold the view that salespeople should always say yes to their customers. I think this stems in part from the old saying, "The customer is always right." I would like to argue that saying no, when it needs to be said, is not only powerful, but ultimately, in the best interest of both parties.

Years ago, I was calling on an outdoor company in Seattle. This company published books, an annual catalog, and a variety of direct-mail products. My focus was on the catalog. While waiting for the catalog project, my prospective customer decided to give me an opportunity to prepare a proposal for its postcards. While this was much appreciated, it can also be a dangerous way to start off. My company was very good at printing catalogs, but while we could print postcards, it was not our strong suit. If I prepared a quote for the postcards and my pricing looked high, the buyer might assume I wasn't competitive and not even give me an opportunity to prepare a quote for its catalog. I decided to take a different path. I decided to say no, gently.

First, I thanked my buyer for the opportunity and told him I would be happy to prepare a quote, but honestly, postcards were not what we did best. I went a step further and told him about a company that specialized in postcards right there in Seattle. This company gathers orders from several different customers and gang-prints them all at the same time, giving customers the best price by letting them share all the setup costs.

My buyer was sort of surprised that I would refer him to a competitor during a live project. I told him my job was to provide the best solution for my customers, even if that best solution was not me.

As I expected, my price looked ridiculous, so the customer went to the other printer I referred him to. In fact, that printer won by such a large margin that my customer called to thank me. He was so glad I had introduced him to this other printer; the company had lots of postcard projects, so this new vendor would save them a lot of money.

Fast forward to the end of the year, it was time to produce their annual catalog. I prepared my proposal, delivered it, and won the project. When I thanked him for the order, he said, "You do know it was always going to you, right?" I responded with a thank you but asked why it was always coming to me. He told me anyone who did what I had done with the postcard order was someone he could trust. He needed vendors he could trust.

The result, I lost the postcard order for $1,200, but won the catalog for $13,000. I then proceeded to print the catalog for three more years. The investment of $1,200 yielded a long-term customer who trusted me and brought me nearly $39,000 in catalog orders over the next three years.

This was a powerful lesson. To this day, when I get a project I cannot produce, or one I can produce but is not a good fit for my company, I either find the customer a better resource and decline to submit a proposal, or I submit a proposal and let the customer know I may not be the best fit in advance. However, when it is the best fit for my company, I go all in!

Asking for the Order

At some point in every sales cycle, there comes a time when you simply ask for the order. This is not simple, but neither is it difficult if you ask at the right time in the right way. Asking too early shuts down the process—usually with no real explanation. Not asking is just as bad. In my experience, buyers prefer to partner with someone who asks for the order. To ask for the order, you have to earn the right to ask.

Asking for the order too early is just like starting to sell too early. If you have not walked through the needs analysis to understand fully what your customer needs, you are not really in a position to ask for the order. Invariably, you ask and the answer is no, with no *real* reason given. Of course, the customer will make up a reason, like your price is too high, it is not ready to make a move right now, or it is staying the course with its current supplier. These are usually excuses to get rid of you without having to tell you that you did not fully understand or address the company's true needs. Nothing you said was compelling enough because you really did not know what would be compelling in the first place.

In short, if you are selling a car but the customer is buying a horse, asking for the order will not help. You will not be seen as a credible professional. You will not be seen as a low-risk option, since you really have not done your homework.

Very early on in my career, I learned a valuable lesson: Sometimes, you simply need to ask for the order. I learned this lesson from a somewhat controversial book titled *Signs for Sexuality*. This book taught deaf high school students, who read lips, about slang—and not just any slang. This book was the definitive guide to terms students may never have been taught, which made lip-reading those terms pretty challenging for them. For example, most schools teach the scientific names for male and female body parts. But, on the playground and in social situations, most teenagers use slang.

When this happens, the deaf student is lost or, at the very least, confused.

This particular job was a $25,000 job. In an era when $100,000 was a good monthly goal, this was one of my biggest jobs to date. I went to the meeting and made my presentation, and then the client said she was probably going to go with a vendor she trusted and had used before.

Dejected, I drove back to the office. I explained to my boss, Bob, how the meeting went. First, he asked, "Did she say no, you will not get this order?"

"Well, not really," I replied. "She simply said she was probably going with a vendor the company currently works with."

"Good," said Bob. "Did she comment on your price?"

"Actually, she did," I replied. "She said early on our price looked pretty good."

"Okay," Bob said. "Greg, here is what I want you to do. Get on the phone, right now, and call her. Tell her you really want this order, and under your supervision, she can rest assured that nothing will go wrong. Then ask for the order."

My first thought was she obviously did not want to work with me. But Bob said, "Trust me; ask for the order. Then you will know either way if it is a real no or a yes."

I did everything Bob told me to do. To my surprise, she paused and said, "Yes, you can have this order." Keep in mind, at this time I had a monthly sales budget of $50,000. Up until then, I had only sold one job for $8,000. At $25,000, this was half my month's sales in one job. This was a big job.

I was floored and the hero of the sales meeting that week. I was the guy who simply asked for the order.

Here's what I learned from this situation:

1. Sometimes you simply need to ask for the order.
2. Do not assume the answer is no.
3. Make it personal; guarantee what you will do.
4. Selling is what happens "after" you reach an objection.

The above illustrates how simple asking for an order can be. As with anything else, many ways exist to ask for the order. Each salesperson must find what he or she is most comfortable with. The following are a few ways I have asked for an order.

- "I think I have addressed everything you requested, can I have this order?"
- "What else do you need from me?" If the response is nothing, then reply with, "Great. Can I have this order?"
- "Am I your best solution?" When the customer says yes, simply say, "Great, can I roll up my sleeves and go to work?"

In some situations, when I cannot get a yes or an order, I simply ask, "What will it take?"

"What will it take to get this order?" is a great question. It's like asking for the order, but it allows the buyer to feel in control and possibly provide you with the missing piece of the puzzle to get the deal done. It's also a powerful way to find out if you are one of the finalists.

As mentioned earlier, every business is different and everyone has a different style. In my opinion, the key to success is to be yourself and figure out what works for you. Don't be afraid to make mistakes and take a few risks; it's how you test to see what works, what does not work, and what is the key to growth.

Never "Un-Sell" Yourself

Or, as I was taught, know when to shut up and leave. It is no secret that some salespeople love to talk. While liking to talk is not necessarily bad, too much talking by a salesperson can be problematic.

In sales, getting a commitment from a customer can happen face-to-face in a meeting, or it can happen via a follow-up phone call or email. Sometimes, when you get a yes during a meeting, it can catch many salespeople off guard. I have actually sat in meetings where the customer says, "We are going to go with your company for this project." And what do you think the salesperson did? Kept selling. In one meeting, the guy kept on talking about his company, the value it provides, the benefit the customer will receive, etc. It was amazing; the salesperson was not expecting a yes, so he kept right on selling.

Here is the problem with this situation. First, it shows you are not listening. You are in sales mode and not about to be derailed by an "award." Second, you are probably in the process of un-selling what you just sold. What should you do? Wrap this damn meeting up and get out. The only thing that can happen is you can turn that yes into a no if you say the wrong thing.

Remember the HMO story? The customer said my proposal was $7,000 higher than the other vendor. I asked, "What does that mean?"

I will never forget his response. "It means you better deliver on time."

I picked up the purchase order, said thank you, and left. Only after I was back at the office did I follow up with a few questions I had. I learned a long time ago that when you get a yes, stop talking.

Once the proposal is in your customer's hands, what's next? In the following section, we will discuss ways to follow up and stay in the game.

Following Up After the Presentation

The proposal is in the customer's hands—now what? This is an area where many salespeople can find themselves in a challenging position. Back in Chapter 7, we talked about leaving a bridge designed to set up a reason for the next meeting. This same concept applies in a more subtle way after the proposal is in your customer's hand. If you managed to leave a bridge, you have a genuine reason for following up. For example:

- If there is a ramp-up time and/or a deadline to meet, it's a good reason to check back.
- If you ask when to expect a decision and get a date, it's also a good reason to follow up on that date.
- If something in your industry is changing that could affect the proposal, that could be a good reason to follow up.
- If you happen to be in the neighborhood, why not stop in?
- If raw materials are about to spike, raising costs, that is a great reason to follow up.

Often, customers are not prepared to make a final decision on the spot in the final meeting. So what now? How do you keep in touch? How do you stay in contact without being annoying? How do you avoid the dreaded black hole of sales when the customer goes dark and stops communicating? Is your competition still selling while you're not? Have you lost the order and the buyer simply does not want the unpleasant job of telling you that you lost? Any sales-person can tell you the feeling of not knowing, or having the boss hound you for the status of a proposal when there is nothing to report. The time after a proposal can be a little frustrating if you don't have a plan of action. So let's jump in and see how to follow up after a proposal to secure the order.

How Long Should You Wait to Follow Up?

No set time exists when it comes to trying to reconnect, but back in Chapter 7, we talked about leaving a bridge, or a reason to come back for a follow-up visit, or at least to stay in touch. This bridge works for both follow-up appointments and when following up after presentations. Hopefully, as you left the meeting or presentation, you did this very thing—you created a reason to follow up. At the very least, it is important before you leave the meeting to ask when a final decision will be made. After a week has gone by, there are a few ways to try to reconnect and finalize the deal.

Has the Customer Gone Dark?

If I find the customer has gone dark and is not responding, I like to get her or him on the phone to ask the "What would it take?" question as discussed earlier. At this point, you have nothing to lose if the customer has gone dark and all you are looking for is closure.

Keep in mind, she or he may have made a decision and simply doesn't want to tell you. In some cases, she or he may be trying to decide and it is taking longer than expected. Always be professional; always be polite. I have had projects awarded to me in one day and some in one month. If you get frustrated and your tone shows it, you could un-sell yourself and not even know.

Creative Follow-Up

If a customer has gone dark, or is not providing any feedback, then you will need to get creative. The process here is sort of like that of the cold call or initial introduction, figuring out how to reach out and connect without becoming a nuisance, or what I call professional persistence. Professional persistence is simply finding ways to be persistent, stay in touch, and keep the lines of communication open. Connecting can be done in many ways, and you will have to find what works best for you. Below are a few follow-up methods I use that you might find useful.

- Call or email to see if there is anything else the customer needs to assist in the process.

- If a tour was not part of the sales process, offer to provide a tour.
- If, in your industry, samples are helpful, send some via FedEx or courier.
- If you have a few references from happy customers, send them over via FedEx or courier.
- If you would like to bring other team members into the conversation, offer this.
- If the customer is a local client, tell her or him you will be in the area on Thursday and would like to stop in.
- If you come across a white paper that is relevant, send that to your customer. Or, better yet, maybe you can write a white paper on the subject to send?

Win or Lose, Now What?

I know this sounds funny, but there are usually two outcomes: you win or you lose. There is a proper way to respond to both situations. Occasionally, there is a third option: there is a delay on the customer's end, and no one wins. In that case, simply stay in touch; it may be a long haul.

If you win, close the process out. Thank your new customer and get the purchase order (or whatever you use) in writing. I prefer to get everything in writing; that way there are no surprises or memory failures. Double-check the details and make sure you have everything lined up both with the customer and internally to kick off the project or process, beginning your new relationship. The key to getting repeat business is to do exactly what you said you would do. Make sure to delight this customer in the hopes that the customer will not only send you more work, but tell others of the positive experience.

But what if you lose? Trust me, you are not going to win every sale, so you had better get used to that right now. Every industry has a win/loss ratio. In my industry, if you win 25 percent of the time, you are doing just fine.

If you do lose, it is imperative to ask for feedback. Many customers will tell you exactly why you lost. Some will just try to get rid of you by saying you were too expensive, but if you are a little persistent, you can usually get more than one reason.

Then you have to decide if the customer is worth pursuing further or if it is time to move on. If the customer still provides an opportunity, then roll up your sleeves and get ready for the next sales cycle and project. If it only has one project a year, you may want to keep the customer in your database, but not spend too much time on it until next year rolls around.

Whether you win or lose, it is critical to document what you learned. Did you win? If yes, why? What did you do that helped you win? Who was your competition? What was the deciding factor? I would not recommend asking immediately after you win. Wait until the job or project is complete; by then you have a relationship. Ask then why you won, and what it was that helped the customer pick you.

If you lost, I feel it is fair to ask the same questions of the customer. If the customer gives you a chance, you could do a sales post-mortem to try to figure out why you lost, who won, and why your competitor won.

The bottom line is, you need to learn from your wins and your losses. I would argue that learning from your losses is more important by far. The only way you can improve is to document what worked and what did not. Then replicate what went well and fix what didn't. This was just one of many sales adventures you will have. The good news is that selling gets easier and success becomes more frequent the more you practice.

Saving the Sale and the Customer

I want to talk about a lesson I learned early in my career so I can pass along some of the best advice I have ever received. Let's say you win, everything works, your customer places its trust in your hands, and you are being paid well to deliver a project. You sign an agreement to deliver a product or service on time. But what happens if, on the first job or project, you are not successful in keeping your promises? In the real world, things do not always go as planned. Sometimes we screw up, sometimes our customers have unrealistic expectations that are not necessarily spelled out in the agreement, and if the customer is not happy, you must fix this. Remember, we are not only looking for jobs or projects; we are looking for long-term accounts. We want repeat customers who say good things about us to other prospective customers. The advice I will pass on is, "Pass the praise and take the heat." After two rough experiences of my own with clients where various mistakes outside of my control caused things to go south, I was at a loss on how to recover.

Once again, I sat down with Bruce, my go-to guy for situations like this. In his office, legs crossed, fidgeting with his glasses as always, he listened to my story. After I had finished explaining the situation, I asked Bruce, "How do I fix this problem?"

I will never forget his exact words. "Pass the praise and take the heat," he said.

Of course, I said, "Excuse me. What?"

"It's simple," he repeated. "Pass the praise and take the heat. If you always remember this, it will serve you well in most situations." Simply stated, when things go well, give credit to your team (pass the praise), but when things take a bad turn, the fault is yours and yours alone (take the heat). I recently heard a quote from a salesperson that makes a lot of sense to me: "I don't care who gets the credit; I just want to win." To me, this is the sign of a true leader, and a good salesperson has to be a leader.

He went on to explain that in both situations, I had done nothing wrong, but I had to view these situations from the customers' point of view. Did I really think the clients wanted to know that Bill ran the press poorly, Karen in bindery folded the signatures crooked, or that

Mike did not realize a wholesale catalog was not designed to be used by the public in a retail environment? Hell no, those sounded like excuses.

It is not a good idea to distance yourself from your company when the company makes a mistake. Think about it this way: When you are developing the relationship, you say *we* can do this, *we* can do that, *we* have great quality, *we* have great customer service. If the minute there is a problem, you start saying, "*They* messed it up, *they* printed it wrong, *they* folded it wrong, *they* used your wholesale catalog and were not supposed to," it doesn't show a cohesive company to the client.

When something goes wrong, that is the time for "I." Bruce went on to explain how to handle it. "On the first project, I want you to get face-to-face with the customer and say, 'I take full responsibility for this. I should have been closer to your project and requested samples at every stage to ensure nothing slipped by. When we first met, I promised you I would manage your project better than anyone else, and I have not. What can I do to make this right?'"

On the second project that had issues, Bruce instructed me to do the very same thing. "Get face-to-face with the owner and tell him, 'I take full responsibility for this. I am not sure how one of your books managed to get used in this way, but it is my responsibility to ensure none of your product is used by our employees. What can I do to make this right?'"

Of course, both pieces of advice were spot on and both ended well. Both customers remained my customers, but make no mistake, they made themselves clear and rightly so. I did take a lot of heat.

I know: What about pass the praise? Well, there is always a flip side. When projects go well or better than expected, never take credit for it. On the first project, if things had gone well, I would have said, "Well, Ms. Customer, don't thank me; it was my team members, Mike and Karen, who produced the wonderful quality."

Pass the praise and take the heat seems like a loss for the salesperson, but it really isn't. "You are your company," Bruce told me. "In good times and in bad, customers will respect this and continue doing business with you if you follow this simple philosophy."

Summary

In this chapter, we have really started what many would consider "selling." We finished gathering the information we needed and moved into the proposal stage. One of the key elements in this stage is the proposal. Remember to make the proposal relevant. If you walked through the needs analysis properly, you should have lots of good, relevant material to use in presenting of your proposal. It is always a good idea to get organized and figure out who your audience is, which format you want your proposal in, and how you plan to deliver it: fax, FedEx, or in-person. In my experience, in-person is always the best option.

We also discussed asking for the order and the power of a fast no. Never be afraid to find a way to say, "Can I have this order?" If they say yes, great. If they say no, you are not done; you just have more work to do.

When you are in the sales cycle, always remember that when you win, shut up, say thank you, and leave. After customers have told you they have selected you, you run the risk of un-selling yourself if you continue to talk. You can always follow up after you have gathered your thoughts. And last but not least, pass the praise and take the heat. Customers love this, and it builds trust.

In the next chapter, we will walk through what to do after you win. You have to perform, and the first job is critical in establishing a long-term customer.

Exercise

1. Take a moment to write down some ideas for how you would prepare a proposal? (Word document, PowerPoint, etc.)

   _____

   _____

   _____

   _____

2. Write down some creative options for asking for the order.

   _____

   _____

   _____

   _____

3. Write down a few proposal follow-up questions that you can use to leave a bridge.

   _____

   _____

   _____

   _____

4. Look at any recent losses you have had and see if you can go back and find out why you lost.

_____

_____

_____

_____

5. If you have a good customer who will share, see if you can find out why the customer chose you? (Only do this after they have been a customer for a while.)

_____

_____

_____

_____

CHAPTER 9
MANAGING THE PROCESS

Rinse, Lather, Repeat!

Whether you won or lost, the good news is that you now understand the process and get to walk through it all over again. Yes, you guessed it; this was just one of many opportunities you will have to grow your business. In sales, you need to have as many of these opportunities in process as possible.

The most important steps:

1. Find, create, and qualify leads.
2. Contact the correct person.
3. Get an appointment or opportunity.
4. Perform a needs analysis.
5. Create a relevant proposal.

6. Ask for the order.
7. When you do get the business, execute.

Note: Again, the key to remember in this process is not to sell too early. If you sell too early, you run the risk of selling something your potential client is not looking to buy.

Creating a Pipeline

At any given moment, you could have a number of opportunities in various stages of the sales process. If you are only involved in one opportunity at a time, this will still work, but it will make growth very slow. In theory, you will be reaching out to new customers, trying to set up new appointments, having appointments, preparing proposals, and trying to finalize the sale on a variety of different opportunities every day.

It is important that you learn to change gears. That simply means at some point during your day, you are calling new clients, following up on meetings you had with other clients, preparing proposals for new clients, and finalizing deals with still other clients. Now, if you are a small business and you are the only salesperson, you may have to balance your time with other duties. It is okay to focus on one opportunity at a time, or multiple opportunities, as long as you have something in the pipeline at all times.

Beware of the Lag

The reason you need to have something in the pipeline at all times is because of the lag. Yes, there is always a lag between that first call to a prospective client, closing the deal, and receiving revenue. In my industry, I have literally started and finished a project in one week, and I have also had projects take as long as a year. The typical sales process is about 30-60 days, so that creates a 30-60-day lag in production, and if your client is on net 30 financial terms, that means you may not see money for 90 days. This is the reason for always having something in the pipeline at different stages all the time.

Beware of the Canyon

As mentioned above, it is critical that you learn to change gears and try every day to keep the sales process moving on every opportunity, including customer outreach and cold calling.

Picture this: In January, you are doing everything right, calling on new clients, following up on other potential clients, making presentations, giving tours…all good things to do to keep the sales process rolling along. Then, in March, you notice the fruit of your labor, and you see sales start to climb. While this is exactly what you want, you need to be aware that taking care of these new clients can suck up a lot of time, unless you have a customer service team that can take over while you continue to sell. Assuming you don't, what happens is that you spend all March taking care of your new clients. Meanwhile, no one is selling. Come April, you look at your sales and see a huge drop-off—or canyon. The problem is you were so busy taking care of your new clients that you stopped selling and stalled the sales process. So you jump back on your sales horse and start selling again. After a short lag, you again experience success and new sales dollars start to flow in May because, as we discussed, there is usually a lag between selling and revenue. I call this pattern the hills and valleys; I also call it a pain in the ass because the volatility makes planning and crewing very difficult. To simplify the concept, picture every other month being good sales months, and conversely horrible sales months in between. This cycle is not always easy to get out of, but to truly grow and run a profitable business, you must find a way to manage your existing customers while continuing your new customer outreach.

Keeping Client Data to Identify Trends

Every process involves data. It is imperative that you keep really good notes at every step of the process for later use. Even if you simply use an Excel database to track all the details for each account, that is better than nothing. If you are not learning from your interactions, you could be making the same mistake multiple times. Plus, if what you are doing is not working, keeping track of all data is the only way to figure out how to improve. If you can afford it, I highly recommend employing a CRM system. Back in Chapter 3, we talked about using technology to keep your efforts organized. If you are a one-person company, you can get by using just a spreadsheet. As you start to grow, add multiple new customers, and add salespeople to your team, you will need a method and process for keeping track of all customer interactions.

As mentioned earlier, many CRM systems are on the market—Salesforce, Microsoft Dynamics, HubSpot, Pipedrive, Freshsales, Zoho—just to name a few. Deciding which one is best for you and your company can take just a weekend of research, which is a nominal investment that will almost certainly add value to your company and enable you to upscale your business with ease.

Preserving Your Sanity

Salespeople can make a lot of money. This is true, in part, because salespeople make a lot of money for their companies, and in part, because it is not a simple job. Up until now, I have not discussed any of the pain that is possible, but I feel now is the time to let you know what you probably already suspect. Sales can be challenging and even outright difficult. But if the reward were not great, the process would not be worth it. You will fail, since no one ever wins every time. You will have people hang up on you before you can even get a full sentence out of your mouth. You will have nice people say no nicely, and you will have rude, mean people say no not so nicely. You must not take it personally, and you should never take no from someone who can't say yes. (Make sure you are talking to the right person.) You cannot let any of these situations dissuade you from your mission. Your company's future depends on your ability to develop a thick skin and wade through each and every no to get to a successful yes.

Throughout my career, I have developed some tricks to help me manage my sales process. Following are a few that might help you:

- **I'm on it.** I was once getting on a plane from Los Angeles to Seattle. Just before I boarded, I got an urgent email request from a customer. I did not reply since there was really nothing I could do while on the plane. I figured I would simply respond after the two-and-a-half-hour flight. Once I touched down, I looked at my email in-box. The person who had emailed me had sent about five more to see if I had actually received the first email. Then I noticed a few similar emails from other clients. That's when I realized I had to have a process that would buy me time and allow my customers to relax. I came up with a campaign called "I'm on it." All this campaign entailed was responding as fast as possible, within five minutes if possible, with, "I'm on it." This did two things: 1) It allowed my customer to relax, know I received the email, and focus on other things, and 2) It also allowed me to cut down on unnecessary redundant emails. This "I'm on it" became so popular that my customers started using it. I once called a customer and all I got back in response was "I'm on it." Turns out they were in an all-day meeting and did not want me worrying all day that my message was not received. I can't tell you all the bizarre times and locations I responded with, "I'm on it," but the good news is that it works and helps everyone involved.

- **I'm in the area.** Whenever I am looking for a reason to visit a prospective customer, I simply say I will be in the area and ask if there is time to see me. Then I back-fill appointments in that area, or I create new appointments to ensure I make good use of my time.

- **Is there anything else you need from me?** Whenever I am looking for a reason to follow up on a proposal under consideration, if I am out of creative ideas, I simply fire off an email asking what else the customer needs from me. This works more often than you would think.

- **Email reminders.** I have many, many customers, so I have developed a foolproof way of not forgetting anything important. I do two things: First, in the morning, I start an email titled "Don't Forget," but I don't send it. Yet. Once I've added enough things I need to do to the list, I send it to myself. If I am out and about, away from my desk, I start a new list. This way I never forget what needs to get done and what promises I have made. Second, when my customer does email me with a request and I am away from my desk, I simply reply, "I'm on it," but I bcc myself so I have a copy of the request.

- **Can I have thirty minutes of your time?** Some customers are difficult to get in to visit with. Sometimes I simply promise to keep my meeting to thirty minutes if they agree to see me. Once they agree, I usually set an alarm on my phone for thirty minutes out of respect. When the alarm goes off, I let them know "You gave me thirty minutes, and I promised to keep it to that." I find this strategy to be quite effective. Oh, and as a side note, I have never had anyone hold me to exactly thirty minutes. In fact, as long as it is going well, they will keep the meeting going. I once had a thirty-minute meeting go two hours, and the customer was the one who kept me there. But I must tell you, you had better be sharing some really helpful, relevant news with the customer if you want to ignore the thirty-minute window.

- **Write the proposal for the CEO.** While lots of legwork can go into a proposal, you should not omit what you have already covered with the buyer, regardless if it feels redundant. Often, a buyer will have to get approval from senior management to authorize a purchase, especially a big ticket item. I always write my proposals as if the customer's CEO, CFO, or Director of Marketing will be reviewing it. Picture this: The CEO has some free time and decides to read a proposal at home one night. There is no one there to answer any questions or clarify, so you had better make sure the proposal contains everything he or she needs to understand and approve it.

- **How does that impact you/your business?** In a question-and-answer session with a customer, every time I hear a problem or issue, I always ask, "How does that impact you or your business?" This is how you get the customer to talk about his or her pain. If you get a customer to talk about his or her pain, you will uncover confirmed needs.

These are just a few of the tricks I use to help get the results I need. I think some of these tricks are how you build your personal brand. It is important that your customers see you as a professional and that you do indeed have a personal brand.

Objections & Obstacles

No book that focuses on sales would be complete without addressing objections and obstacles. Whether you are calling someone for the first time, making a presentation, or signing a contract, objections will always be raised at every step of the process. To win, you must address all of these objections. I like to view objections as questions from the customer, nothing more. That helps me roll up my sleeves and go to work without taking it personally. A few common sales objections:

- **Your price is too high.** While this statement can be true, it is often an excuse to get rid of you. Obviously, customers usually won't tell you their current pricing, so you have no way to know if your price is really too high.

- **My Approach:** I like to ask questions like "Compared to what?" or "What part of my proposal is too expensive?" or "How high am I?" or "Who is providing you that price?" or "Are they delivering everything you want for that price?" or "What if I can match their price? Would you give me an opportunity?" I find if you ask good questions, you can usually break down this objection.

- **I am happy./The status quo is fine.** Again, this statement is usually a way to get rid of you quickly. Or the customer really doesn't see a need to make any changes.

  - **My Approach:** Ask more questions: "What problems are you experiencing?" or "Do you have a backup supplier in case your primary supplier has a problem?"

- **Trust.** Often, a customer who just met you won't trust you. This is not a bad thing—it is a natural thing. You have to assume if you are a brand new solution, you are an unknown and untested solution. Customers won't come out and tell you they don't trust you because that would be rude. But you have to assume with a first-time customer, at a first-time meeting, with a first-time project that the customer doesn't trust you. This assumption is usually correct.

  - **My Approach:** Ask for clarification, ask for an example of a trust issue, demonstrate how your other customers place trust in you, and carefully offer guarantees that you can actually pull off.

- **Fear of Change/Risk.** Change is scary. Most customers will not tell you they are scared, but often with the right questioning, they will share their fears. "The last time we tried a new vendor, it went badly," or "The product is mission critical," or "If I get this wrong, I will get fired."

  - **My Approach:** It is your job to allay these fears. Make promises you can keep, guarantee results you can guarantee, show examples of similar situations with other customers you have worked with that turned out well. Also, never be afraid to show them that not changing can also be a risk in itself.

- **Bad timing.** Timing is never good, so this is usually a brush-off.

    - **My Approach:** Ask why. Or "When would be a good time?"

    - **I need to review with my team.** If you get this response, it could be an honest response or you may have missed a step in the process. Decision by committee is not good, especially if you know only one of the team members on the committee.

- **My Approach:** You should always know who is making the decisions, but even if you don't, you have to stay in the game. Ask to present to the team; ask to get the team in for a tour; ask who is on the team. This response is usually a sign your customer wants to say no, but is looking for a way to do it. By asking to speak to the team, you are testing to see if this is the real reason and possibly getting your foot in the door.

- **Just send me some information.** This usually occurs over the phone, and while it is a brush-off, it does not mean you are done.

    - **My Approach:** I always agree to send information, but before I do, I need to ask a few questions to ensure I send the customer the correct materials. I also follow up to make sure the potential customer did indeed receive the information. Doing some research never hurts. When you send information, you should try to address some needs or pain you think the customer may have. This process can be a long haul, but if you are persistent, you may prevail.

- **I'm in a contract with my current vendor.** This response is usually given on an initial call. While it is sometimes true, it is often just a way to keep a salesperson from calling repeatedly.

- **My approach:** My first question is to ask when the current contract is set to expire. I always put a note to follow up in my CRM or Outlook calendar a few months in advance of that date so I am early, not late. I always tell the customer I will be here next year since this is a career, not a job. Keep in touch in ways that make sense for your business. Tell the buyer you are happy to be a good backup in case the current vendor ever has a problem.

- **I'm not interested.** This response is a way for a busy gatekeeper to get off the phone.

  - **My Approach:** Unless the person says this and hangs up, say, "All I'm looking for is an opportunity to show you something you probably have not seen before."

- **Call me back in a few months.** This can be a legitimate response or a brush-off.

  - **My Approach:** Again, ask questions. "Okay, I will call you then. Will you be looking for proposals then?" or "Is there anything in the meantime I can send that would be helpful?"

- **Difficult Gatekeepers.** Every office has people between you and the contact you are trying to reach. If you get the brush-off from a gatekeeper, such as a receptionist, administrative assistant, etc., this is no place to stop.

  - **My Approach:** Again, don't take no from someone who can't say yes. Find a way to get to the person you know is the correct person. If the receptionist is challenging, try calling at lunchtime. Often someone fills in for the receptionist at lunchtime. This fill-in person may be easier to get around. Send FedEx packages to the person you want to reach. Typically, those are private and the person they are addressed to opens them. Also, instead of a FedEx package, a 9 x 12 business envelope nicely addressed and mailed or hand-carried is usually intriguing. FedEx is usually seen as commercial; a standard white envelope is more intriguing.

These are just a few of the many different types of objections, rejections, and obstacles you may face. It is always a good idea to plan ahead for all of these and have a response ready. If you do a little pre-call planning and address any and all objections you think you might encounter, it can make a phone call and an appointment much more profitable because you will look like a professional who is prepared. One thing you can never do is give in to frustration or get angry. You must be professionally composed at all times. If the customer can rattle you in a phone call or in a meeting, you will not appear to be a professional worthy of the customer taking a risk with, and you will never obtain equal business stature.

The next book I write will be all the things I wished I could have said to rude clients but never did. It will be a long book.

Persistence Requires a Positive Mental Attitude

One way I like to look at rejection, obstacles, objections, and outright rude people is this: If I have done my homework, and I am pretty darn sure the customer is a good fit for what I do, but he is saying no, then he or she is really just saying "Not now." Here is where persistence comes into play. At some point, you have to qualify the customer, but to accomplish that usually takes getting in to evaluate the situation. So you must be persistent until you decide that maybe the customer is not worth the effort. Know when to push and know when to walk away. Another way I like to approach these challenging situations is to remind myself that all these excuses mean the customer is probably protecting his or her current vendor. If he or she is being loyal to the current vendor, some day he or she will be loyal to me. Stay positive.

Making Mistakes

As I have always said, "Anyone can sell and everyone should sell." But no one is born with all the necessary sales skills—they must be learned. Never forget: You will make mistakes, just like I did in the following example.

Early in my career I made the first of many mistakes. The mistake was worth $3,000 on a $10,000 project. While I was new, I understood that a mistake of $3,000 pretty much ensured we were not going to make any money and we may even pay for the privilege of producing the project.

I received a call from Bruce, my boss and the company owner, to come to his office and discuss something. Naturally, I was a little fearful. I was just out of college and in my first job, so I was afraid of actually being fired for the first time in my life.

When I got to Bruce's office, he had me sit in that familiar chair. It was one of those chairs you would see at a conference or seminar—silver metal frame with cloth back and seat. I was familiar with that chair since I was often in Bruce's office. I liked trying to pick his brain so I could learn quickly. However, today I was not there by choice; I was there to take a beating.

Once I arrived, I could see the billing statement on top of the job I had managed to screw up. It looked like one of my high school English papers with red ink everywhere.

Bruce asked me to explain what had happened and why. So, right then and there, I laid it all out: what had happened, why it had happened, what the result was, and why there was not a simple fix to prevent the $3,000 loss on this job.

For a moment, Bruce sat, planning his always thoughtful response. Here are his exact words: "Greg, if you are making mistakes, that means you are pushing and trying new things, and that is good. If, however, you start making the same mistakes over and over, you are not paying attention, and that is not good. Part of becoming a professional requires a few mistakes along the way."

From this experience, I learned:

1. Success requires some failure.
2. Reward effort as well as success.
3. Teachable moments—look for them.

Shortening the Sales Cycle

First, let's define the sales cycle. From the time you find a lead until the time you get an order from that lead as a new customer, that is the sales cycle. In some industries, that can be a day, week, month, or year. Each industry is different, but for simple transactional sales, the cycle tends to be shorter, and for larger ticket items or complex sales, the sales cycle can be quite lengthy. Regardless, the shorter the sales cycle, the faster the money is flowing into your bank account.

One of the challenges we all face is shortening the sales cycle. As you can imagine, searching for leads is challenging. These are cold leads requiring initial calls to introduce yourself. The problem is every cold lead not only has to be found and contacted, but it also has to be qualified. It does no good to pursue a lead if he doesn't buy what you sell, and getting leads qualified can take time.

As mentioned earlier, you can simply ask existing customers for referrals. However, there is another way, assuming you already have some customers: Mine your own customer data to figure out what "industry vertical" you are currently in.

What is an industry vertical or market vertical? A vertical is a specific industry like automotive, healthcare, or publishing. Within each of these vertical or market vertical industries are groups of customers. To sell to an industry or market vertical, you simply develop a go-to-market strategy tailored to that specific industry. If you are focusing on the publishing market, you develop a lead list and a game plan to call on all publishers you find in that vertical. As you can imagine, when you are talking to leads in publishing, healthcare, and the automotive industry, the same approach is probably not going to resonate with all of them. You must develop a unique approach for each one.

For example, each of these customers buys printing. Heck, nearly every business does. But they do not all buy the same type of printing, they do not all use printed materials the same way, and they all have different ways of buying.

Again, I will use my print sales background to illustrate the power of industry or market verticals.

I started my current job back in 2014. Like every sales executive, my goal was to move from the starting salary to full commission compensation as quickly as possible. The only way to do this was to shorten the sales cycle. The only way to do that was to call on pre-qualified leads.

Early in my new role, I went through our company's customer database. I made a quick list in an Excel spreadsheet of the companies we currently worked with, what industries they were in, and what products we produced for them. It took a good weekend or two to get it all nailed down, but once I had the data, I was able to sort it by industry. I identified thirteen industry verticals in total. Once I had this, I then did the calculation to see which companies we did the most and least business with. (See Figure 3.)

Industry Verticals	Number of Customers
Magazine Publisher	11
Wholesalers	10
Insurance	10
Banking	6
Book Publisher	2
Sports	2
Education	2
Food Retail	2
Manufacturing	1
Entertainment	1
Research	1
Travel & Map	1
Non Profit	1
	50

Figure 3: Industry Verticals Based on Our Top 50 Customers

In Figure 3, you can see each of the thirteen industry verticals and how many customers we had in each one. Why did I make this list, and how did it help me?

1. We had a lot of brokers or wholesalers in our customer mix. This tells me that our pricing is pretty darn competitive. If a wholesaler can take our price, mark it up, and resell it against other printers, with no middle man involved, that is pretty impressive.

2. It showed me where, as a company, we focused our selling efforts—wholesalers, magazine publishers, Insurance companies etc. Note: Two of these four require you to be the lowest bidder to win. Again, the idea that we are very competitive is reinforced.

3. It also showed me where we have less focus, but still had some success. This told me where the opportunities were.

Technically speaking, I am an expert in every industry vertical above, right? What I did was to focus on the industry verticals where we had the fewest customers. For example, I chose book publishers, travel/map, and education. All of these were on the lower end of the grid.

- For the maps, I looked up five good leads, sent out information, and landed two map customers.

- For the book publishers, I looked up three West Coast book publishers and landed one new publishing customer, which happened to be the third largest comic book publisher in the world.

- For the education category, I looked up five universities and landed three of them as customers. They happened to be major universities on the West Coast.

Why did this work so well and so quickly? The answer is quite simple. I reached out to each of these potential customers to let them know we specialized in maps, books, or educational institutions.

In my communications, I wrote and talked about the desire to show them how we helped other customers, just like them, produce better-printed materials and save money at the same time.

In short:

1. I knew these leads were good leads because we already worked with similar customers.
2. I knew how to speak their lingo. I could talk the talk.
3. I had samples and examples of happy customers I could leverage in my selling efforts.
4. I could demonstrate that I understood their business.
5. I had instant credibility since I worked with others in their industry.
6. I was a subject matter expert in their industry.

7. I was a low-risk option. If others in their industry trusted me, they could too.

Note: To wrap all these into one, I was relevant. Everything I said and did was relevant to their business.

So which of the following is a better opening line when talking to a technology company?

1. Thank you for taking my call. I was wondering if I could arrange a meeting with you to talk about your printing and distribution needs.

2. Thank your taking my call. I was wondering if I could meet with you to show you some of the solutions I recently implemented for Microsoft and Hewlett-Packard, and the positive impact they had on their businesses.

It's not hard to tell which of these opening lines would get the best results on the phone. If you are looking to shorten the sales cycle, this is the best way. Why reinvent the wheel? Why start from scratch when you can literally have traction immediately by demonstrating your expertise in a given industry? This is not rocket science. You would be amazed at how many people don't take advantage of it.

Practice, Practice, Practice

To some, this entire process of selling may seem daunting, time-consuming, and downright scary. Many want to know how long it will take to see results and how long it will take to get good at it. Keep this in mind. The only difference between the soccer legend, Pelé, and me, is that he has more touches on the ball than I do. Now that may seem egotistical, but I truly believe that with enough practice, whether it is soccer or sales, anyone can learn enough to make a huge impact. Just like soccer, or anything else, becoming successful at sales really takes lots and lots of practice.

Summary

In this chapter, we talked about managing the process after your new customer has bought from you or placed an order. Remember, once you have successfully on-boarded a new customer, the process starts again with another customer. (Rinse, lather, repeat.) Ideally, you would like to have many customers in the pipeline in various stages of the process to keep the new business sales flowing. Managing different leads in different stages of the sales process requires you to "change gears" or do a variety of things every day. Always remember from a cash flow and crewing point of view, depending on your business, the "lag" and "canyon" can impact your business, but the more new opportunities you have, the less this problem will affect you.

We also talked about colleting customer data. Never underestimate the power of good, relevant data on your accounts. Also, we discussed your sanity, objections, obstacles, persistence, and mistakes. All will be your companions on the sales journey, and while not always easy, they are part of the process.

In the following and final chapter, we will wrap up with strategies and ideas to get you in motion. It is critical that you get started on your journey today. Remember, in the small business world, procrastination is not your friend.

Exercise

1. This chapter assumes you have just sold to your first customer. Make a list of the first three new customers you would like to approach in the next thirty days.

_____

_____

_____

_____

2. Look at your business and the typical sales cycle from new customer to money arriving in your account. What is your sales cycle?

_____

_____

_____

_____

3. How many new accounts would it take to fill in some of your current canyons (slow months)?

_____

_____

_____

_____

4. Make a list of the data you think would be helpful to know about all your customers. How will you gather it?

_____

_____

_____

_____

5. Make a list of the most common objections you currently get and prepare an answer for all of them. (As you get new objections, add to the list.)

_____

_____

_____

_____

CHAPTER 10
WRAPPING UP (Q & A)

How to Get Started—Today

We have almost reached the end of this book, but not the end of your journey. Actually, just the opposite—you are beginning your sales journey. This book was written to help lead you through the process of selling on purpose, protecting your dream, and realizing the rewards that owning a small business provide. Here are the next steps to actually start the process.

1. **Relax:** Realize you are in a marathon, not a sprint. What you don't know, you will learn as you go. Will there be fear and pain? Of course. Will there be success? Absolutely. But relaxing and moving through the process with confidence is always easier.

2. **Create a Plan:** Each plan is different, but as someone once told me, "Without a map, any road will do." So take some time to

think about what you really want to communicate to your market and your potential customers when you meet them. What is important? What is different? Why you? You must create at least an outline of your plan and your vision. What will it look like when you are done? Some would argue an outline is not enough detail, but I also think it is important not to get too wrapped up in documenting everything. Often, you can get so caught up trying to cover every detail and eventuality that you never really get out and get started. Remember, you don't have to launch everything all at once. In fact, I would suggest you don't.

3. **Create a Timeline:** Once you have what you need to get rolling, I always suggest you create a timeline and list milestones along the way, making sure to attach dates to them. I also recommend writing down your goals as part of your plan or timeline. Having a target is always helpful.

4. **Gather Leads/Targets:** Once you have a plan, a timeline, and goals clearly written down, start building leads. Whether it's by using Hoovers, ReferenceUSA, or list purchasing, start amassing a list or lists of prospective customers you would like to reach out to. The more you have, the better. Nothing says you can't do this as you go, and you will, but when you have a good supply of leads upfront, it helps you get into the routine and keep going.

5. **Exercise:** Okay, I know this may sound funny, but I am a firm believer in blowing off steam in sales. I have been a member of my local YMCA for nearly twenty-five years, but I have belonged to a gym my entire life. You will find that sales is not easy and will always have its ups and downs. To me, you have to find a way to burn off that frustration and celebrate success. A good workout is the best medicine. This is just my humble opinion.

Common Sales Questions

Finally, to end this chapter, here are some questions I'm frequently asked. The answers to them may help you in your specific situation.

1. **My company is busy and making good money without a sales process, so why should I consider sales outreach?**

   While I am always happy to hear this, I cannot tell you how many times in my career I have seen companies doing well one day, and then something changes. It can be something within your company, or it can be an external event like a new competitor moving into town, a large customer going out of business, or new local regulations affecting your business. The bottom line is that when things do go south, that is not the time to try to build a sales process. You need to build it slowly and steadily and make sure it is in place if, or when, you need it.

2. **How long does it take to create a sales environment or sales process?**

   There is no single answer to this question. It really depends on you and what your needs are. If you start off small and build, you can see some results pretty fast. If you take on too much too fast, you may have some growing pains. I would say starting small and building as you go is probably the best way to go. This is why it is best to start this process before you have a huge shortfall in revenue or problems you are trying to solve.

3. **Can I build a sales process with a company of only three people?**

   Absolutely! In fact, you can start with a company of one. Remember, selling is as much a state of mind as it is a process. Start small and add as you grow is always the safest way to begin moving in the right direction.

4. **Do I have to have a particular personality to sell?**

   Nope! Sure, if you are a gregarious, life-of-the-party sort of person, this can make the outreach process a little easier. But remember, some of the smoothest, slickest salespeople can come across as slimy or insincere. Some of the best salespeople I know are pretty quiet.

5. **What are the benefits of inside versus outside salespeople?**

    This is a really good question. Again, the answer really depends on your market and what your product is. Inside salespeople tend to be a little less expensive, since outside salespeople usually work on commission. But in some industries, it is critical that your sales folks visit your customers. In other industries, there is really no need for a full outside salesforce or salespeople. It boils down to the cost and the benefit, which each business must weigh.

6. **What are the benefits of having your own salespeople versus selling through distributors?**

    One of the biggest benefits is control. If you have your own sales team, you can lead and control the process. If you are relying on another organization to sell your products, they will not be as committed as you are. If they do the same thing for other customers like you, will they give you the attention you deserve? How do you handle customer service if your team is not there for the initial sale? Again, you can have your own sales team or use a distribution network. Both can work well; it just depends on your particular needs.

7. **If you had to name one thing that is helpful for a small business starting a sales outreach program, what would it be?**

    Honestly, I would say just getting started. Many want to wait until they need to generate more revenue quickly, but that means you are in a rush. Starting early and simply doing something little every day to keep moving in the right direction is critical.

8. **What are the biggest mistakes made by owners building a sales process into their companies?**

The three most common mistakes owners make are: 1) Trying to roll out a complete sales department all at once. 2) Hiring a salesperson and expecting immediate positive results. 3.) Waiting until the company is in financial trouble to develop a sales process and/or team. If you need new revenue immediately, you probably waited too long. But nothing is impossible; you just need to hustle.

9. **Do you have to pay salespeople commissions?**

Not always. There are salespeople on salary, salary plus commission, and full commission. I have also seen salary plus bonuses for hitting sales targets. It really depends on what your industry and business looks like. To attract talent, commissions need to be enticing. Some feel that 100 percent commission (no salary, bonuses, or draw) is the only way to properly motivate a salesperson. While motivation is a good thing, if you have the right people in the right positions, it can work either way.

10. **How much should I pay in commission to a sales rep?**

Again, this depends on how your business and costs are structured. You have to do the math to figure out what you can afford and calculate what the additional business is really worth. If you have a product with a high value-added component, it is easier to find room for commissions.

Summary

Like anything new, it takes time to get into a rhythm. But the only way to get into a rhythm is to start. I'm sure you may have other questions that haven't been answered in this book because everyone's situation is different, but hopefully these answers will get you started, and you can always reach out to me if you need additional help. You'll find my contact information at the end of the book.

Exercise

1. Pick a date when you want to make your first outreach call. Make it realistic because you may have a little work to do to prepare.

   _____

   _____

   _____

   _____

2. Ask yourself, as a busy small business owner who is now adding "sales" to your duties, what will you do to burn off the stress of selling?

   _____

   _____

   _____

   _____

3. What is your biggest fear; what will stop you from starting? Figure this out and fix it, or call me, and I will help you fix it. Today is the day to start.

   _____

   _____

   _____

   _____

4. Make a list of how many customers you would like to add in the first twelve months.

_____

_____

_____

_____

A FINAL NOTE

PUTTING IT ALL TOGETHER

Okay, now what? We have come to the end of the book, but in all honesty, you are just beginning your journey. This book was written to help lead you through the process of selling on purpose, protecting your dream, and realizing the rewards that owning a small business provide. The question is: What are you going to do now?

I would like to propose a challenge to you to start your journey *today*, this very moment. Procrastination has no place in sales. As with any other book, seminar, or training, the information I've offered here will only help if you actually start the process. Knowledge itself is pretty useless unless you apply it in some fashion. You can read all the books in the world on how to be a great soccer player, but until you take a ball and get on the field, you will never grow or progress to becoming comfortable with the ball at your feet, and you will never fully gain the skills until you practice. You just have to start trying and things will develop.

So, let's begin. On the lines below, list the ten things you will commit to doing to start this process over the next thirty days. (It is okay to go back to Chapters 1, 2, and 3 if you like to refresh yourself on the process.) While I say thirty days, some to-do items will be easier to start than others. Honestly, I suggest creating a To-Do List and knocking off some of the simple items first to get some momentum—things like create a tagline, create a value proposition, gather lead lists, start compiling leads, ask your customers why they like working with you, research your competition, etc. It is easy to get stuck in the perpetual rut of learning and planning and never actually apply what you have learned, so get moving now.

1. _____

2. _____

3. _____

4. _____

5. _____

6. _____

7. _____

8. _____

9. _____

10. _____

As you have navigated your way through this book, you have learned about a process that will help you achieve the goals and objectives you have for your business. You have learned how to:

- Define what your product really is and how to talk about it.
- Develop a Go-to-Market Strategy that works for your business.
- Create a sales process/platform within your company, even if you are a company of one.
- Find out where your customers live.
- Generate leads lists.
- Make initial contact.
- Get-in—set an appointment.
- Get an opportunity.
- Execute the sale, gain agreement.
- Manage your first project.
- Follow up after winning your first project or after losing your first project.
- Get repeat business from your new client.
- Fine-tune the process to become more efficient.

Again, until you apply these new skills and start walking through the process, these are just words on a page. Trust me, I started off as a young college graduate twenty-eight years ago with nothing— just a desk and a phone—but it only took me fourteen months to see amazing results. If you truly want to grow your business, then all you have to do is roll up your sleeves, commit to working at it every day, and give it a go. If you apply the skills, tactics, strategies, and ideas routinely, then you will be well on your way to growing your business, protecting your dream, and making more money, *without the fear.*

Now that you have read my book, I would like to invite you to provide any feedback you feel would be beneficial. Like you, I am always looking for ways to improve and refine my process and now this book, so tell me what you liked, what you disliked, what subject I spent too much time on, or what subject I should spend more time discussing. I would also like to hear more about your challenges, frustrations, and/or your successes. To encourage you to reach out to me, I would like to offer you a free, no-obligation 30-minute consultation to discuss any issues or challenges you are facing. This consultation can be via phone, Skype, or Google Hangouts. I am here to help. Contact me via text or email and we can set up a quick call. My personal contact information is:

greg@smallbusinesssaleswtf.com

206-769-3974

My mission is to help small business owners like you by showing you how to grow and protect the business you built without the fear often associated with sales. Remember, "Anyone can sell and everyone should sell." I look forward to hearing from you so we can talk about the success and prosperity that will surely follow once you take action based on what you learned in this book.

Here's to your success!

SALES RESOURCES

Books

Adamson, Brent. *The Challenger Sale.*

Altschuler, Max. *Hacking Sales.*

Bayan, Rick. *Words That Sell.*

Bettger, Frank. *How I Raised Myself to Success in Selling.*

Bird, Tom. *Brilliant Selling.*

Bistritz, Stephen. *Selling to the C-Suite.*

Bray, Cory. *The Sales Enablement Playbook.*

Burg, Bob and John David Mann. *Go Givers Sell More.*

Cardone, Grant. *The 10X Rule.*

Carnegie, Dale. *How to Win Friends and Influence People.*

Cassell, Jeremy. *Brilliant Selling.*

Covey, Stephen. *The 7 Habits of Highly Effective People.*

Dixon, Mathew. *The Challenger Sale.*

Doerr, John. *Insight Selling.*

Eades, Keith. *The New Solution Selling Fieldbook.*

Gitomer, Jeffrey. *The Little Red Book of Selling.*

_____. *21.5 Unbreakable Laws of Selling.*

_____. *The Sales Bible.*

Hill, Napoleon. *Think and Grow Rich.*

Holmes, Chet. *The Ultimate Sales Machine.*

Hopkins, Tom. *How to Master the Art of Selling.*

Klaff, Oren. *Pitch Anything.*

Konrath, Jill. *Agile Selling.*

_____. *Selling to Big Companies*.

Mandino, Og. *The Greatest Salesman in the World*.

Marriott, J. W. *The New Strategic Selling*.

Michalko, Michael. *Thinkertoys*.

Miller, Robert B. and Stephen Heiman. *Strategic Selling*.

_____. *The New Strategic Selling*.

Parinello, Anthony. *Selling to VITO*.

_____. *Think and Sell Like a CEO*.

Pink, Daniel. *To Sell Is Human*.

Port, Michael. *Book Yourself Solid*.

Rackham, Neil. *SPIN Selling*.

Read, Nicholas A. C. *Selling to the C-Suite*.

Richardson, Linda. *Perfect Selling*.

Robbins, Tony. *Money-Master the Game*.

Roberge, Mark. *The Sales Acceleration Formula*.

Rosen, Keith. *Coaching Salespeople into Sales Champions*.

Ross, Aaron. *Predictable Revenue*.

Schiffman, Stephan. *Cold Calling Techniques*.

Shultz, Mike. *Insight Selling*.

Sobczak, Art. *Smart Calling*.

Sorey, Hilmon. *The Sales Enablement Playbook*.

Thull, Jeff. *Mastering the Complex Sale*.

Tracy, Brian. *The Psychology of Selling*.

Tuleja, Tad. *The New Strategic Selling*.

Tyler, Marylou. *Predictable Revenue*.

Vaynerchuk, Gary. *Jab, Jab, Jab, Right Hook*.

Watkins, Michael. *The First 90 Days*.

Weinberg, Mike. *New Sales, Simplified.*

Ziglar, Zig. *The Secrets of Closing the Sale.*

Sales Training

Action Selling - *www.actionselling.com.*

Advantexe - *www.advantexe.com.*

Aslan - *www.aslantraining.com.*

Carew International - *www.carew.com.*

Dialexis, Inc. - *www.dialexis.com.*

Double Digit Sales - *www.doubledigit-sales.com.*

Impax - *www.impaxcorp.com.*

Integrity Solutions - *www.integritysolutions.com.*

Janek Performance Group - *www.janek.com.*

Kurlan & Associates - *www.kurlanassociates.com.*

Mercuri International - *www.mercuri.net.*

Miller Heiman Group - *www.millerheimangroup.com.*

RAIN Group - *www.raingroup.com.*

Revenue Storm - *www.reveneustorm.com.*

Sales Performance International - *www.spisales.com.*

Sales Readiness Group - *www.salesreadinessgroup.com.*

Selling Energy - *www.sellingenerg.com.*

The Brooks Group - *www.thebrooksgroup.com.*

The Power to Sell - *www.richardson.com.*

Unboxed Technology - *www.unboxedtechnology.com.*

Value Selling Associates - *www.valueselling.com.*

Vantage Point - *www.vantagepointperformance.com.*

Wilson Learning - *www.wilsonlearning.com.*

Additional CRM Solutions

Act! Essentials - *www.act.com.*

AllPro Web Tools - *www.allprowebtools.com.*

Apptivo CRM - *www.apptivo.com.*

Avidian - *www.avidian.com.*

Base - *www.getbase.com.*

Bluenose - *www.bluenose.com.*

BoomTown! - *www.boomtownroi.com.*

BPM Online - *www.bpmonline.com.*

Buddy CRM - *www.buddycrm.com.*

Bullhorn - *www.bullhorn.com.*

CampaignerCRM - *www.campaignercrm.com.*

Capsule - *www.capsulecrm.com.*

Commence - *www.commence.com.*

Contactually - *www.contactually.com.*

GoldMine - *www.goldmine.com.*

GreenRope - *www.greenrope.com.*

Hatchbuck - *www.hatchbuck.com.*

Highrise - *www.highrisehq.com.*

Infusionsoft - *www.infusionsoft.com.*

iSEEit - *www.now.iseeit.com.*

LeadMaster - *www.leadmaster.com.*

Maximizer - *www.maximizer.com.*

Method:CRM - *www.method.me.*

Microsoft Dynamics CRM - *www.microsoft.com.*

Microsoft Outlook - *www.microsoft.com.*

NetSuite CRM - *www.netsuite.com.*

Nimble - *www.nimble.com.*

Nutshell - *www.nutshell.com.*

Odoo - *www.odoo.com.*

OnContact - *www.oncontact.com.*

Pipedrive - *www.pipedrive.com.*

Pipeliner - *www.piperlinersales.com.*

PipelineDeals - *www.pipelinedeals.com.*

Podio - *www.podo.com.*

Sage CRM - *www.sagecrm.com.*

Salesnet - *www.salesnet.com.*

SalesNexus - *www.salesnexus.com.*

SAP Digitral CRM - *www.sapstore.com.*

Snapforce - *www.snapforce.com.*

SugarCRM - *www.sugarcrm.com.*

TeamWox - *www.teamwox.com.*

Vtiger - *www.vtiger.com.*

Workbooks - *www.workbooks.com.*

ABOUT THE AUTHOR

Greg Andersen was born and raised in the Pacific Northwest and graduated with a degree in Communications and a minor in Industrial Psychology from Western Washington University. While attending Western, he financed 100 percent of his college tuition, books, and living expenses by working a full forty hours a week at a local printing company while carrying a full load of college credits. Hard work and finding a way to make things happen are not new to Greg.

Greg's first foray into sales began while working his second job at Nordstrom Rack selling ladies shoes during seasonal sales events. While he enjoyed the interaction with customers and the money he could make, he was not sure he liked the passive nature of simply waiting for clients to come into the store. If no one came in, he just milled around in the back of the store waiting for an opportunity. Instead, Greg decided to find a sales career where he could use his creativity to build a customer base by seeking out and "bringing in" customers.

Upon graduation, Greg leveraged his practical experience in printing with his degree in communications and went to work in the sales department of Valco Graphics in Seattle. With this full commission opportunity, the amount of money to be made or the number of customers to serve depended on Greg's ability to find new customers. Greg was given twenty-four months on salary to get up and running and then transition into full commission sales. Greg made the transition in fourteen months, and he never looked back.

Over the last twenty-eight years, Greg has spent his time building, cultivating, and nurturing his client base, resulting in many long-time customers in a variety of industries. Among Greg's unique strengths are his uncanny abilities to dig up new business, uncover customers' needs, and provide solutions that create long-lasting value.

To this day, Greg still finds digging up new customers the most enjoyable part of his job. At fifty-three, when most are managing their existing accounts or "book of business," Greg is still out finding new accounts. This passion and the advice from friends are what led Greg to write *Small Business Sales, Without The Fear*, so he could share his secrets and his process with small business owners around the world.

ABOUT THE SMALL BUSINESS SALES INSTITUTE

The Small Business Sales Institute (SBSI) is a sole proprietorship founded by Greg Andersen. SBSI's mission is to reach out to small business owners to help them understand the important role sales or New Business Development plays in the success of micro-, small-, and medium-sized businesses that want to grow. Understanding how to talk about your business is the first step to learning about sales and selling effectively for your business. As a sales professional, Greg is keenly aware that people like to learn and be supported in different ways. The following are different ways you can work with Greg to better understand and learn about the sales process so you can acquire new customers and grow your business.

Book:

Small Business Sales, Without The Fear was written as a do-it-yourself simple read that lays out the entire sales process from end to end so that anyone can work through it at his or her own pace. By following the steps outlined in the book, anyone can learn enough to sell on purpose and find new customers.

Seminars:

SBSI also puts on seminars intended to gather a group of business owners and walk through the process in a one-day seminar. Having a variety of people from a variety of businesses all learning about sales brings a whole new dimension to learning about the sales process. What you will discover is that the fundamentals of sales are very similar in most businesses and only require small tweaks to tailor them to your industry.

Coaching:

For those not comfortable in large groups, those experiencing serious revenue problems, and those simply wanting some one-on-one coaching, Greg is available. Greg's coaching process involves a quick survey of your business and writing an action plan for you to follow. Regular, ongoing contact and advice is part of this process. But Greg is quick to point out that he will not sell for you. He will teach you how to sell and set up a repeatable sales workflow for your business.

Speaking Engagements:

Greg is also available for speaking engagements. Whether it is a small or large group, Greg has unlimited energy and is passionate about motivating small business owners to take control of their destinies and not only start growing their businesses, but also protect those businesses by consistently adding new customers.

Greg can be reached at:

206-769-3974

greg@smallbusinesssaleswtf.com

gregorywandersen@gmail.com

NOTES

NOTES

NOTES

NOTES